The Treasury of White Trash Cooking

Ernest Matthew Mickler
and Trisha Mickler

With color photographs by the author

Ten Speed Press
Berkeley • Toronto

Ten Speed Press
P.O. Box 7123
Berkeley, California 94707
www.tenspeed.com

Cover design by Toni Tajima, based on a design by Jonathan Greene
Cover photos by the authors
Interior design by Jonathan Greene and Jeff Brandenburg

SPECIAL EDITION

First printing, 2002

Printed in the United States of America

The Treasury of
White Trash Cooking

*"You got the good ingredient,
You got the good thing."*

— *Aunt Emma*

"It was the most magnannygoshus day, ever. Edna Rae loved sayin that when the weather was good. . . You know as well as I do, if Edna Rae hadn'ta been in that box, she'da been on Saunders' Dock a-fishin."

CONTENTS

FOOT WASHINS,
PRAYER MEETINS,
CREEK BAPTISMS,
AND ALL DAY SINGS

CONNETTA'S DREAM

Lou May Witkins screeched to a halt right in front of Iris Maxine Dove's house. They were the best of friends and she couldn't wait to get inside and tell her the very latest. Lou May made a fast slide out of her car. She fixed herself up. Shifting here and there and a nonchalant pull at the back of her skirt to make sure the 'goat was not in the pasture'. Her friend was constantly reminding her of that. Iris had already parted the curtains and was watching.

But, by this time, Lou May had lost all her patience and started screaming Iris's name way back at the street. Iris met Lou May at the stoop and helped her get in quick, cause she could tell it was the 'low downest' piece she'd heard in a long time. Iris could always depend on Loumie (she called her that) to bring the very 'worst' right to her kitchen table. And Iris specially knew it was Thursdays, today, that Loumie had her regular weekly standing appointment at Oleen's Beauty Shop.

Loumie didn't even say hello, just rushed straight through to the kitchen and squirmed-down in a yellow-bottomed, pearlized dinette chair. Iris had already poured her a cup of strong coffee when Lou May said, "Iris, I've heard it all now. You cain jus go on an kill me and bury me cause I heard it all."

Iris, forgetting to compliment her on one of Oleen's finest hairdos and lavender-pearl rinse jobs, didn't play games or waste time. She asked her, straight out, which dryer she was under.

"I was under number three," Loumie said.

"That's the one which makes an awful racket. You cain't hear right, under that thing. Are you shore you heard it all, exactly?" Iris asked.

"Well, I finagled it until I got one of my ears free from it so as I didn't miss a word. But she HAD already started," Loumie said in a not-so-sure way.

"OH! Honey, your ear shows it too, it's red as fire," Iris came back.

"That ain't necessarily from the heat of the dryer, darlin, I want you to know that for shore," Loumie shot back just as quickly.

"Well I know who's there with you on Thursday, so it's got to be on Marrabelle Shuster." (Loumie's face didn't register.) "Or, Connetta Boyle." (Iris could tell that was the jackpot.)

"Iris you scare me. I think you got one of them see-all minds or something," Loumie said, kind of bewildered.

"An if it's about Connetta" Iris came right back, "it's got to be a good one. Cause you know what they say about anybody that gits her hair dyed that awful purple-red color, plus wearin them open-toed things on their feet. An what mother do you know, would let her young'uns go barefooted 'fore May 1st or 'fore the dew dries. She just beggin for ground-itch."

"Well, it's true and I know you're plenty right," Lou May said. "But I got to hand it to Oleen, she listened to the whole story and didn't flinch a hair. She even laughed a little. An I made positive that I kept my nose stuck in my National Enquirer. I helt it up so high there was noway they could see my free ear."

"Enough of the preliminaries, Loumie, now git own with it. You done flusstrated me," Iris piped.

"Just hold your taters, Iris," she said, and without further priming lit into the story:

"Well, it seems Connetta's been goin to that Holycostal Church over in Itta Bena, the one where they do everything from snake hanlin to speakin in farun tongues. And she told Oleen, right while she was dabbin at her roots, that this secret society had picked her to wash the preacher's feet right after the actin out of the Last Supper."

"Well . . . she does kinda look like that Mary Magdalene with all that hair an everything," Iris added. "But that secret society, I can tell you that was the preacher himself."

"Now, first of all, how do you know what Mary Magdalene looks like, and what makes you so shore the preacher's the picker all by hisself?" Lou May questioned.

"She's all over the Bible pitchers and she's in every play," Iris declared, "and they ain't many of 'em around that can turn down a chance like that. She's carryin a sign. . . . . them open-toed shoes. Plus that power them preachers has got over people, some just use it like the devil."

"I know you're right, but it just gripes me to think of it,"

Loumie squenched. "Enough of that. We'll do the judgin later on," she said, as she continued the story:

"About that time, Oleen chuckled when Connetta told her that the preacher suggested, since it was like a play, maybe they ought to have a little rehearsal on the side. I mean it was different from the rest of the thing, was her exact words she told Oleen. She said the preacher said she didn't need to bring a thing."

Iris broke in, "I bet he did. I wonder what he'd a done if she coulda left her you-know-what home. That woulda froze his monkey."

"Now be quiet, Iris, er you gone mess up the story," Loumie said before getting back to where she was:

"She told Oleen that she'd never been to a foot washin before and didn't know what on earth to expect. So she said she put a perfumed-up old washrag in a little baggie and stuck it down in her pocketbook just in case. An don't you dare say what you thinkin, Iris, the story's bad enough as is. She got to the church at the specified time, tried the door but it was locked. The preacher was right there though, so he let her in and relocked the door."

"I bet he did," Iris slipped in.

"Shut up Iris. Quit buttin in. I'm the one that overheard all this," Loumie said, kind of exasperated, but went on telling Iris, "It's a downright dirty dog rotten shame people's got to ack like that."

"Ack like what, darlin, you ain't told old Iris nothin yet?"

"Well, I hope to God I don't have to spell it out for you, cause I ain't usin the language Connetta used on poor Oleen," Loumie said.

"Poor Oleeeeeeen!!! Honey, she's heard everything they is to hear an then some, an take an turn that wrong-side-outereds an she's bared witness to that too," Iris ranted. "They hear it all from who's gotta itch where to who's a scratchin it —an with what!"

"Well, I've listened to it all now," Loumie continued:

"She told Oleen that it went fine and nothin much happened till they got right down to the ackshul washin of the preacher's feet. She said he had this big enamel basin filled up with water, sittin at the foot of a chair, square in the middle of the church platform. But he had his own washrag. So she didn't need to use hers. But when Connetta started washin at his feet, he beginned to laugh like a crazy man, an every time she felt of his feet he'd go goofy on er. It went on like that for a while and finally, she told Oleen, she just quit cause she couldn't hold on to his feet anyways. Then, he set off to outright beg her to tickle his feet some more. An she said he wasn't just askin, he was beeeeeeeggin, honey. At first, she said, she didn't. But he kept on pleadin at er till she couldn't stand it. So, she took that rag an worked . . . his . . . feet . . . over. She told Oleen she thought she'd have to get the okgegon tent to revive 'im."

Iris was squealing in her seat and Loumie knew she had her goin' so a little mischief at this point wouldn't hurt a thing:

"Right then, while she was wrenchin that mess outta her hair, Oleen asked er, at the real foot washin, not the rehearsal, what did them Itta Bena ladies bring to eat?" Loumie went on, taking the story to an abrupt turn.

Iris didn't stand still for it and said, as if she was going to choke Loumie, "You are pullin my leg! With Oleen's appetite for dirt, she'da never asked Connetta any such thing in the middle of that kinda story —or your hair ain't purple". . . . . "Oh God, I didn't mean that Loumie! I meant Connetta's hair. Yours is just a shade darker than it usually is."

But it didn't faze Loumie, because she had decided where she was going with the story, so she just went on with the list of dishes the ladies from the Itta Bena Holycostal Church had brought to the foot washin. "Connetta said they had greens and beans, corn breads and corn pones, dumplins, stews and casseroles. They had Spam, ham, an fried pork chops. Pies, cakes and a puddin or two."

"Okay, Loumie, we know what them ladies from Itta Bena eat, now git back to the story," Iris said hopefully.

Loumie, still with devilment, continued, "She told Oleen that about that time her and the preacher tumped over backwards and rolled and wiggled and squirmed all over that platform and, then, the preacher made his lunge. . . . ."

"Oh . . . my . . . god . . . Iris, is that clock right. I don't believe it. I got to git home and start my supper. I had no idea it was that late!" She grabbed her pocketbook and ran for the door.

Iris didn't move. But, she thought, if she could have gotten her hand on Lou May Witkins head, she'd have pulled all of her almost-purple hair out! But, instead, she'd have to call Oleen to get the rest of the story, even though they were still on the outs over another cross-wired story from under dryer number three.

AUNT SARAH'S STEPPED ON CORN BREAD

> Alabama ground cornmeal
> Enough hot water to make a mush
> Plenty bacon drippings

Make pone. Bake 2 or 3 hours at 250 degrees.
    Aunt Sarah said, "Careful you don't hurt your foot."

GAYNELL'S TATER TOES CASSEROLE

2 lbs ground beef
1 large onion, chopped
1 can Campbell's Cream
  of Mushroom Soup
1 can Campbell's Golden
  Mushroom Soup

1 soup can of water
1 2-lb package of Tater
  Tots or 2 1-lb
  packages

Fry down the beef and onion. Add the soup and water and mix thoroughly. Pour the Tater Tots over the top and cook at 475 degrees for 25 minutes.
    Gaynell said, "This'll restore your energy after washin all them feet."
    Serves 6.

AUNT JENNY'S COMPANY'S COMING CASSEROLE

1 lb ground beef
2 8-oz cans tomato sauce
½ lb cottage cheese
1 8-oz package of Philadelphia Cream Cheese, softened
¼ cup sour cream

⅓ cup green onions, chopped
2 or 3 Tbs chopped green pepper
2 Tbs melted butter
12 oz thick, flat noodles, cooked and drained

Cook the ground beef until browned. Stir in the tomato sauce. Combine cottage cheese, cream cheese, sour cream, green onions, green pepper. In a two-quart casserole spread half the noodles, cover with cheese mixture, then cover with the rest of the noodles. Pour on the melted butter, cover with the beef-tomato mixture and bake uncovered in a 375-degree oven for 30 minutes.

"Will serve as many as you can," she said.

FOOT POTATO SALAD

4 cups cooked potatoes, cut into chunks (if you lined 'em up it'd be about a foot of 'em).
4 hard-boiled eggs, chopped
1½ cups sliced celery
¼ cup sliced radishes

½ cup sliced green onions, including green tops
1 cup mayonnaise, Kraft
1 Tbs apple cider vinegar
1½ tsp salt
2 tsp French's yellow mustard
½ tsp celery seed

Mix together the first five things. Thoroughly blend the mayonnaise, vinegar, mustard, celery seed, and salt. Pour over potatoes and mix with your hands. Chill and it carries good.

Serves 6.

TRUE GRITS CHILI

6 medium onions,
  chopped fine
6 medium green
  peppers, chopped fine
2 garlic cloves, minced
4 lbs ground beef
4 16-oz cans tomatoes
  with juice
5 16-oz cans kidney
  beans, drained

2 cups cooked grits
2 6-oz cans tomato paste
1 cup water
1 tsp apple cider vinegar
3 whole cloves
2 bay leaves
4 or 5 Tbs good chili powder
  (Maxene's, if you can
  get it)

In a skillet brown the onion, garlic, and peppers in oil until golden. In another skillet, brown the beef in batches. Drain off fat. Mix the beef and onion together in a large pot and add the tomatoes, beans, grits, tomato paste, water, salt, vinegar, cloves, chili powder, bay leaves, and black pepper, to taste. Cover and simmer one hour over low heat. Add a pinch of sugar. Simmer uncovered for another hour. Take out the bay leaves and cloves (hope you can find 'em all) before serving.

If it's right off the stove it'll say hot for an hour. Serves 20.

OLEEN'S STUFFED PEPPER SLIPPERS

8 green peppers
1 cup cooked rice
1 Tbs Crisco
1 lb ground beef

¼ cup chopped onion
¼ cup chopped green
  pepper
1½ tsp salt
½ tsp pepper

Cut tops off peppers and remove the pepper seeds. Put peppers into boiling water and cook 2 minutes—don't overcook. Drain. Melt Crisco in a skillet and add ground beef, onion, chopped pepper, salt and pepper. Brown and add rice and mix. Stuff peppers with mixture and place in baking dish and bake for 30 minutes in a 350-degree oven. Serves 8.

CONNETTA BOYLE'S COLE SLAW

1 head cabbage, shredded	½ cup bees' honey
1 onion, chopped	½ cup apple cider vinegar
1 green pepper, chopped	½ cup cooking oil
1 3-oz can pimientos	2 tsp sugar
	2 tsp salt

Mix together the cabbage, onion, pepper, and pimiento. Combine remaining ingredients in a pot and bring to a boil. Pour dressing over the cabbage mixture and mix well. Cover and refrigerate for 3 days.

Careful when you take the lid off, cause sometimes it'll smell like old feet.

Serves 10.

PRAYER MEETIN PUNCH

2 quarts of good sweetened tea	1 6-oz can frozen limeade
1 22-oz can canned orange juice	1 6-oz can frozen pink lemonade
1 6-oz can frozen pineapple juice	

To the tea, add the frozen juices and then stir in the orange juice. Chill and let sit till your throats are dry.

Serves 16.

PREACHER'S CHICKEN KETCHA-COLA

> Fryer
> Bottle of ketchup
> Bottle of Coca-Cola

Cut up your chicken just like for frying and salt and pepper it a lot. Put all of it in a skillet at the same time. Cover it with a whole bottle of ketchup—the size hamburger stands have on the counters—then pour in a bottle of Coca-Cola (no substitutes, please) and cook it over medium heat till it's done. You can sorta flake meat off the bone with a fork when it's done and it looks like barbecue sauce. You can tell if it's not done by tasting it.

MOCCASIN BRANCH SKILLET CAKE

1½ cups flour	2 tsp vanilla
¾ cup Crisco oil	1 cup pecans, chopped
½ cup buttermilk	1 cup sugar
1 egg	1 tsp salt
2 tart cooking apples, peeled and sliced	1 tsp baking soda

Combine all the dry things in a big bowl. Add what's left and thoroughly mix. Grease up a cast iron skillet and pour in the batter. In a 350-degree oven cook for 40 to 50 minutes.

Tastes even better if you can dangle your feet in the branch while you're eatin it.

MARY MAGDALENE'S ARSH POTATER SALAD

1 lb cooked Arsh
   potaters, cubed
3 hard-boiled eggs,
   chopped
¼ cup ripe olives,
   chopped

3 Tbs green pepper,
   chopped
1 cup sliced celery
1 onion, diced
½ cup mayonnaise
2 Tbs French's mustard

Combine mayonnaise and mustard. Mix the other ingredients together and pour dressing over, mixing thoroughly. Season with salt and pepper to taste. Chill. Doubles and quadruples real good.
   Serves 4.

MARY LOU'S DEVILED-UP COLLARD GREEN SURPRISE

1 loaf corn pone or corn bread (a little smaller than a shoe box)
2 cups of leftover collards, including liquor and fatback
1 tsp yellow salad mustard

A. Scoop out center of corn pone. Reserve for corn bread and milk.

B. Dice fatback, if pieces are large and return to collards.

C. Mix collard greens, mustard and just enough of the pot liquor for a soggy but not soupy consistency.

D. Fill corn pone with the collard mixture. Let sit a few minutes, slice and serve.

POTTA COLLARDS

2 bunches of collards
Fatback or ham to season
Salt and pepper to taste

Pick out and strip the leaves from the tough stems. Wash 'em to death to get rid of the grit. Takes about 3 to 4 washings. Fry out the season meat till you get a little fat from it. Drop in the collards by the handful and cover. If pot is too small, fill it and let them wilt, then there's plenty of room for the rest. When all is wilted, add enough water to cover. If they a real strong greens and smell bitter pour off the first water and add more. That cuts down on the strong taste. Simmer till tender, add a pinch or two of sugar and cook ten more minutes.

HOT PEPPER CABBAGE

1 head cabbage
Season meat
3 hot peppers

Sear season meat and peppers in a dutch oven. Cut cabbage into quarters and add. Cover and cook till tender. 15 or 20 minutes. Add water if necessary.

OLEEN'S BEAUTY PARLOR POUND CAKE

1 cup Crisco
2½ cups plain flour, sifted
½ cup self-rising flour,
    sifted

2½ cups sugar
5 eggs
2 tsp vanilla
1 cup milk

Blend Crisco and sugar for 10 minutes. Add eggs one at a time. Beat each time for one minute. Add milk and vanilla and flour and blend well. Bake in tube pan for one hour at 325 degrees. If necessary, let cool.

MARY MAGDALENE'S NEVER FAIL POTATO ROLLS

1 pack yeast
1 cup milk, lukewarm
1½ lbs cooked potatoes
¼ cup shortening

2 eggs, beaten
1 tsp salt
Flour
2 tsp sugar

Dissolve yeast in lukewarm milk. Whip potatoes, add yeast, sugar, shortening, eggs and salt. Add enough flour to make a soft dough. Let rise till doubled in bulk. Roll out half inch thick and cut with biscuit cutter. Spread with butter and fold over. Let rise an hour and a half. Bake at 450 degrees for 10 to 12 minutes.

MT. NEBO MOCK LOBSTER SALAD

(No Seafood in Recipe)

¼ lb crackers
1 sweet green pepper, diced
1 cup celery, diced

2 hard-boiled eggs, chopped
2 cups tomato juice
1 cup mayonnaise

Crumble crackers, add remaining ingredients and mix. Tastes like lobster but there's none in it.

Crackers should be in rather large pieces.

SLUICEY-DAB IN A FOOT TUB

1 head lettuce, large	Salt and pepper
Duke's mayonnaise	1 large cucumber
Sour cream	1 large onion
Cider vinegar	1 good-sized tomato

Shred lettuce thinly. Thinly slice cucumber and onion. Chop up tomato coarsely. Throw together in a large bowl or foot tub. Add sour cream, mayonnaise and cider vinegar until the vegetables are covered probably about a quarter inch—the salad should be rather thin and "sluicey"—soupy. Amounts are probably about 2 pints mayonnaise to one half pint vinegar and one pint sour cream. (That's a guess.) Lots of salt and pepper to taste. You'll know when it's right. Runny, soupy, and wilted. It's better from the icebox. And even better left over on sandwiches.

STEAM FRIED CORN

Cut corn off cob. Brown bacon in cast iron skillet. Add corn and some water, at least 2 tablespoons, but no more than half a cup. Steam fry approximately 3 minutes on medium heat or until water is just about gone. Put a piece of tinfoil on it and in the cooter shell it goes.

LOUMIE'S ORANGE SLICE CAKE

2 sticks margarine	1 tsp baking soda
2 cups sugar	1 lb orange slice candy
4 eggs	1 small box dates
3½ cups plain flour	2 cups pecans
½ cup buttermilk	1 can coconut

Cream margarine and sugar. Add eggs one at a time. Dissolve soda in buttermilk and add alternately with flour. Cut orange slice candy and dates in small pieces. Roll nuts and dates and candy in small amounts of flour just to coat each piece. Add all ingredients and mix by hand. Bake at 250 degrees for 2½ hours. When cake is done leave in pan and pour glaze over top and let cool in pan.

Glaze: blend together well one cup orange juice and 2 cups powdered sugar.

CONNETTA'S REHEARSAL COCONUT PIE

2 cups sugar	⅔ cup buttermilk
4 eggs	2 tsp vanilla
1 stick margarine or	1 can coconut
butter	Unbaked pie shell

Mix all ingredients together and bake in unbaked pie shell at 325 degrees for 30 to 35 minutes. And that's about as long as Connetta's interest runs.

MARLENE'S HONEY PUMKIN PIE

1½ cups steamed canned
    pumpkin
¾ cup honey
¾ cup brown sugar
¼ tsp nutmeg
½ tsp salt

1 tsp cinnamon
½ tsp ginger
¼ tsp cloves
1½ cups evaporated milk
½ tsp vanilla

Mix ingredients in order given and bake in one crust. Sprinkle with nutmeg before baking. Bake at 425 degrees for 15 minutes, then 350 degrees for 45 minutes. Cool.

MAYBE MORE SQUASH CAKE

4 boiled squash (maybe
    more)
1 cup milk
3 cups sugar
1 tsp vanilla
2 eggs, scrambled up
    (but don't cook 'em)

1 block butter
3 cups flour (maybe
    more)
3 tsp baking powder (½
    tsp more for each
    extra ½ cup of flour)

Mix everything except flour and baking powder. Then add flour gradually. Maybe more, if you need it. Add baking powder (remember to add extra if you use more flour). Bake at 350 to 375 degrees for one hour.

FUNERALS,
WAKES,
AND CEMETERY
CLEANINS

ONE SIDE OF A CONVERSATION BETWEEN GRACIE DWIGGERS AND ROSETTA BUNCH ABOUT EDNA RAE'S WAKE AND FUNERAL, OVER THE PHONE

"Hello. . . . . Rosetta, that 'ew?. . . . . Yeah, it's Gracie here. Willard Lynn tol me you called. . . . . That's jus what I reckoned you was a callin about . . . . Yeah, Rosetta, I was so sorry you was outta town last week, durin it all. But, you can rest ashore I'm gone fill you in on the particulars. You boun ta heard a few of 'em, by now. . . . . Yeah, I figgered so. But, Rosetta, you wouldn'ta believed that wake a hers. . . . . Now, you stop me when I get ahead a myself. Can you hear me good? Cause, I want to start right at the beginnin, when she passed on, okay? . . . . Well, I was home and they called me to say it'od happened. Now, we was all kinely suspectin such a thing, but still, it jus like ta twisted me to pieces. . . . . Yeah. We was close as sisters. I loooved that Edna Rae. But I realized, quick as hot grease, I had to git a holt on myself. So I did. I thew all six a my young'uns in the backseat of that ol' jalopy a mine and headed dreckly over there, cause, I knowed full well, the famly'od be hungry and tired by the time they got back from the hospital, and all that torment. So, I got to Edna Rae's in about fifteen minutes of the time they called me. But, when I drove up, by the gas pumps in front a her store, I saw Reatha Faye, on foot, splittin them woods behind there, wide-Gawd-dawg-open. She had a apern on an it looked to me like it was filled with some kinda stuff, cause she had it all bundled up in the front like when you pick a mess a peas er sumpthin. At firse, I thought I's seein things. . . . . Yeah, it's plum snakey-lookin back there too. But, I'm absolutely positive, it was Reatha. I could tell er anywheres. . . . . Now, I didn't go through the store. I couldn't bare it, right yet. T'me that store WAS Edna Rae. So, I wen on round to the side and opened up the livin room door. Back behind there, where she lived with Flynt. Rosetta, I cain't remember whether you was here then, or not, but that's the same place she raised all them boys a hers 'fore she married him. . . . . Yeeees, that's right. They ain't a one of 'em that can stand 'im, neither. But that Edna

21

Rae, honey, shorered'n hell, liked 'im. I guess that's natural of 'em, uh? . . . . Well anyways, I wen on in to straighten things and cook 'em some supper. I's doin it, mainly, for Edna Rae and the boys, of course. An I got this, kinely like a . . . a . . . cole shiver on me. Like somethin was wrong. It was, as if, Edna Rae was tryin to tell me somethin. I could see that, as shore as I'ma talkin in this telephone. So, I eeeasied on in and started lookin aroun, when I foun there weren't nairy a pitcher left on that little whatnot stan she had sittin over in the corner. And, her bedroom was stripped, too. All the family pitchers was gone from er bureau. That Reatha Faye, had come in there while everybody was gone and just cleeeeaned house. . . . . She just raaaked 'em off with er arm, right in er apern, looks like to me, and took off out the backdoor. That's when I drove up and seen er goin. They ain't no way we can prove it, but you know, as well as I do, what she had bunched up in there, runnin thataway. . . . . Nooooo Rosetta, it weren't groceries. An the family album's gone, too. Can you b'lieve that. Edna Rae's close frien ramshackin er house, 'fore they could git er to the undertakers. Now them boys, won't have one pitcher of their Mumma. . . . . Ain't it! . . . . Ain't it! . . . . You right, Rosetta. That's jus what she is, no matter how you spell it. She's gone git hers. But what really keeps a-naggin at me is, how on earth'od she find out Edna Rae'd died, right egsackly, when she did. . . . . Yeah. . . . . Yeah. You got it Rosetta, and I ain't had to put a word in yo mouth, neither. You hit it on the sof spot. He double-dawg didn't want the boys to have a one a them pitchers of er, outta pure meanness. They was in cahoots together. That's what they was. Heeee called er an tol er to do it. He's anuther'n whose gone git his, an you can pencil that in, too. I always did wunder bout 'em anyways. But Rosetta, you ain't heard nuthin yet! It gits thick as Miss Fayda Mae's gravy.". . . . .

Just about then, Willard Lynn's patience wore out and he couldn't listen to another word. So, he flipped up his Lazy Boy, as if he was driving it, and splurted out, "Gracie, you better git off that phone. They's five more on that party line might wanta use the thing." Gracie cupped her hand over the mouthpiece and snapped back, "Okay, Willard, don't you start. All they do is listen, anyway.

They don't ever tawk on the damn thing. All of 'em scareder'n biddy shit of it."

Without a pause her hand came off the receiver and she continued. "I'm sorry Rosetta, Willard was a houndin at me. He cain't stan it when I'm enjoyin myself. Anyways, I cooked supper for 'em an we tawked a bit. I was jus gittin ready to leave, when, a knock come on the door. I had a feelin who it was, since she's always the first one at every death. With her biiiig pot of perlow. An 'specially, if it's a widderer. . . . . Yesss, you rite. It was Naireen Sikes in the tightis clothes you ever witnessed. Ol Big Ruby Dukes calls er, right to er face, too, "Naireen The Perlow Queen, Tightest Clothes I'd Ever Seen." She don't miss a chance, that Ruby. But let's do credit to er. . . . . Now Rosetta, don't be ugly. Naireen's always there. And she ain't never failed at makin the best, damn perlow in these scrubs, maybe 'cept for poor ol' Edna Rae. Now, that must mean sumpthin, these kinds a times? . . . . But, Rosetta, you wouldn'ta believed it. Fore I could git the kids piled back in that car and git on, the food started a gatherin. That side porch was like a parade of Sunday dinners for about an hour. . . . . Well, first Naireen, then Jeweldeen Buck, ta'reckly here comes Big Ruby Dukes, and it wadn't long after that 'fore Lucille Collins showed up with her two boys a luggin a washtub. Thank Gawd, it didn't need to be put in the box. . . . . Yeah, it was cole drinks. But you see me, like I am, I was shore it had beer stuffed down under the ice. . . . . Of course it did. Tell me I don't know Lucille Collins, or my name ain't Gracie Dwiggers. Rosetta, I ain't never saw so much food. It jus kept a pourin in. You'da thunk the Pope 'ad died. . . . . Yeas. . . . . n while we on that, you know they ain't nuthin juicier n church gossip. An you was aware 'at Edna Rae was a converted Catholic, wadn't you? . . . . I thought so. . . . . Yeah honey, her first husband was and she wadn't and didn't join', neither. But when he died she raised them boys by the book. Edna Rae always said she took them vowels and she was gone keep'em. Yeeeears later, she went on down there and changed over. But, what went and stirred the water the wrong way was, when she married Flynt, against just about everybody's good advice, he was a divorced man. And you know what them Catholics think a that. . . . . They, flat out, wouldn't bury er in the church, cause of it. But, they said they'd send a pries to the cemetery. Can you imagine that. As I see it, the way she raised them boys and all, they shoulda honored er for that, even, if she'da done nothin else the rest of er life. Which, she, Gawd rest er soul, did plenty more. An uhnotherthing, honey, whether she did or hadn't did, whatever it is, they said she didn't do, ain't no reason to keep her from the Lawrd, if that's what she wanted. Ta me, as hoooly as them fellers might be, I ain't sayin one way er another, but, I'm tawkin, when it comes . . . right . . . down . . . to the gate, they ain't noway they cain git her in, and shorereden hell cain't keep her outta, heaven. But, Rosetta, at that gate's the only time where I can see it'd really matter. . . . . Oh, I'm sorry, Rosetta. I got own it again. . . . . Thank gawd Willard didn't hear me. . . . . Oh yeah, they did send one, Rosetta, but the poor thing was so old he didn't know whether HE was comin or goin, much less understan his english. But we overlooked all that, cause it was the most magnannygoshus day, ever. Edna Rae loved sayin that when the weather was good. . . . . Ain't it. . . . . Cause, you know, as well as I do, if Edna Rae hadn'ta been in that box she'da been on Saunders' Dock a-fishin, certainly not in church or at a funeral home. We alllll knew that. . . . . Rosetta, are you there?. . . . . Rosetta, you've done gone and let me git ahead a myself, after I asted you to stop me. Now, where was I? . . . . Oh yeah, thank you. The food was jus pooooourin in. I never seen so many different kinds of deviled eggs in my life. . . . . Yeah, everybody's hens had ta been a layin double. Well, I crammed it all in Edna Rae's icebox till I couldn't git another mouthful in it and I took the rest home. Cause I knew they'd need it later on. Now, I can tell you, they was some gooood food. . . . . it bein her wake and all. Everybody fixin for it knowed it was gone be helt up to Edna Rae's cookin standards. So, it had to be mouthwaterin. . . . . Like I was sayin, I packed the icebox, and strung it out all over the tables. Rosetta, there weren't a spare inch left. Well I tol 'em all goodnight. And I got outta there quick as I could, 'fore them tears started runnin'. . . . . It's that nighttime what gits you and makes it hardis' to hold on to yourself. But honey, if I'd had a inklin of what was to come, I'da took me a pill and not waked up till waaaaay on inta nex week. . . . . Just . . . hold . . . own . . . Rosetta. I got to catch myself. When I tell about it, I don' know whether to laugh or cry. But, knowin Edna Rae, as I did, I'm shore she'da done a little bit of both. Do you remember how, when somebody tol a joke, she useta cross er legs to keep from peein?. . . . . Oh yeah, she loooved them jokes. . . . . And was full of 'em too. Well, all I can do now is just hope and pray she'da laughed with us on what took place the nex' day. An I feel shore she woulda, after she got over the shock. . . . . But even, Edna Rae'd a had to tax er funny bone to git to that point. . . . . Well, I didn't go right over the next day but I did send two a my girls. They little but they can cleeean, honey. T'ward evenin Willard Lynn went and got the girls 'fore they brought Edna Rae on back home. Meanwhile, I dug down in my closet and foun my funeral frock, hat and shoes and put 'em on. Then I put on my face. No, Rosetta I wear the whitest powder I can find. After that I put on my eyes. A little rouge cake on my cheeks, so I don't look like I'm dyin, and no lipstick. . . . . Why-ay? It's too wicked lookin at a time like that. But I was dressed by the time they got back, so we headed straight on over there again, 'fore the people started coming. When I walked in, I couldn't b'lieve the food that'od showed up durin the day. And someone had gone to the church and borried foldin chairs and spreaded 'em all over the house. Down at the end of that looong livin room Edna Rae was laid out in her coffin. They was two big buckets of yard flowers on each end, somebody'd brought. And the two big floor lamps that them undertakers cain't have a funeral without. . . . . Yeah, they tol me one time them lights made it look 'other worldly'. I ain't shore I like that, specially if it means what ta hell I think it does. . . . . Yeah, you right Rosetta, it was Phillis Willis with that yard full of flowers she's got. It was real pretty. But I was itchy to git on and do my respecks 'fore anybody else got there. Private, like. So, I eased up, said a little prayer and talked to her. . . . . Yeah, just as natural as could be. . . . . Like, she was sleepin. So at peace. But they was sumpthin wrong. Sumpthin that bothered me . . . I think it must a been er hair . . . toooooo done up. Seems to me, they always over fix 'em. Well, I helt on to myself, that time, cause I knew I had to run the show. An I'm so glad I paid my visit when I did. . . . . Cause, just as the sun went down the people started arrivin in twos n threes. I swear to Jehovah, some of 'em was already goose-eyed when they got there. . . . . I don't know why, Rosetta, they haf to be all lickered-up to go somewhere. . . . . Like hell, it never'od work, Rosetta. That Lucille'd done set up a full-fledge bar on the back porch, where nobody that didn't want to, couldn't git seen. Then, on about black-dark, the house got crowded. All the women took over the inside, as usual, and was eatin house outta home. An empty chair wadn't to be foun. And the men had took to the yard, smokin, drinkin, tellin jokes and lord knows what all. But you can imagine, cain't you Rosetta. . . . . Yeah, Reatha Faye was there. Just spinnin an twirlin an a flittin like sumpthin sent from heaven. . . . . Nerve! . . . I never'od seen such a thing. Well, honey, they all got dawg drunk 'cept for the family, of course, and started mixin and minglin together. It was hard to keep the place lookin decent with all the cups, drinks and plates scattered ever-which-a way. But we tried. . . . . I was real proud of them boys, too. They was takin it real good. Flynt claims he got tired of it all, so he went and sit on their bed. Well, everybody, naturally, just followed 'im, 'specially Reatha Faye. . . . . No honey, Naireen was an angel. I watched after er like a hawk. She was the biggest help to me. . . . . Yeah, I tol you, you could depen on her. But Reatha had some outfit on that was as gauzy as it was gaudy. Looked like she was the one bein buried. An she placed herself, on the bed, right nex to Flynt. Now, I ain't judgin nobody for puttin their hand on anybody's knee, but I'll always wunder if it was the right time and place for Flynt to do that to Reatha Faye, even though, they was, all, close as pinfeathers and the bedroom was filled with people. However. . . . . Rosetta, I ain't Claudette Cahill and Chestine Butler. . . . . They was juiced-up to their gullets and didn't like what they seen one bit. . . . . No, Rosetta, they ain't no bloodkin. They just inlaws from waaaaay-back. . . . . Yeah, troublemakers. Well them-two went

into the awfulist cussin streak you'd ever heard come from anybody's mouth, not even ol Big Ruby Dukes coulda top 'em. An it
was aimed right at Reatha and Flynt. I knew what was comin nex,
and shore nough, Claudette grabbed Reatha Faye right by that
great big pone a teased-up hair and started pullin. Chestine latched
on to a handful of dress like a bulldog, just a-snatchin as hard as
she could. Everybody scattered, tumpin over everythin in sight. So,
I ran to the coffin, closed the lid and stood right by it. The tussle
finally ended up out in the yard. . . . . Yeah, you right
Rosetta. If you gonna fight . . . the yard is the place. But the thing
about the thing, thank Gawd, was the boys had already gone off
to spend the night, you can understan that, when it all broke
loose. . . . . Yeas, that was a blessin. So by now, they
was fallin, tumblin and pullin each other all over her flower beds,
till you couldn'ta tol who was fightin and who wadn't, if you'd
wanted to. An cars was diggin outta there like it had been raided.
Finely, Edna Rae's nephew, who's a debady sherff, ran to his car and
turned on the sighreen and flashin light and stopped the whole
thing in it's tracks. . . . . I had a feelin you'd wanta
know that. Well, she looked a mess . . . like she'd been put
through a wringer. As they always say, honey, the feathers was
pulled. But she didn't have a scratch on er. Now them other two
was scraped up one side and. . . . . yeah, they always
do more damage. . . . . cause they wind up fightin
each other. . . . . Honey, Claudette and Chestine will
paaay to fight. It don't matter who it is. They'd jump a Bush
Hawg. But I must say, Rosetta, and don't you repeat this, I was
secretly on their side. . . . . I know I ought to be
ashamed of myself but I ain't. . . . . Yeah . . . by then,
we was egghausted and just about everyone was gone. Them that
wasn't, all pitched in and cleaned the place. You cain't imagine . . .
Rosetta, that front yard of hers looked like the hawgs had got in an
wallered it down. . . . . Oh yeah. The funeral went
fine. You never seen a soberer bunch, not even in a Baptist church,
Rosetta. But, you know as well as I do, somebody had to go show
their behin that day, too. . . . . Yeass, right in front of
a five mile funeral, Big Ruby Dukes leaped out of the car she's a
ridin in and jumped on the back of the debady sherff's motorsickle

and, away she goes, on to the cemetery, clingin to the back of that thing with er dress justa flyin. But that's Ruby Dukes. . . . . Ain't that the truth, honey . . . they ain't no changin it. Rosetta, I got away from the wakenight and I wanted to tell you what I did. Then, I got to go, else, you know who'll be screamin again. As usual, me and Willard was the last to go home. But 'fore I did, I went back in there, lifted the lid and tol Edna Rae I was so sorry it'od hap'emed that way. But, you know Rosetta, she had this, kinely like, peaceful little smile on her face, it looked to me like. And I coulda sweared I heard er say, "Don't worry 'bout it, darlin, I been through a whole lot worser'd'en this.". . . . . Rosetta. . . . . are you cryin? I didn't mean to upset you, honey, but the truth is the truth. Now, I gotta go 'fore I git skint alive. Bye, bye honey. See you t'morrah. Oh! Wait a minute! Wait a minute. This ought to cheer you up a little bit. . . . . Yeas, honey, Reatha Faye brought them pitchers back. Said she was watchin 'em for Edna Rae and the boys. . . . . You don't think I know that, Rosetta. She got a taste a the Devil at the wake and got scared. . . . . She still looks a little be-shovelled to me. Bye . . . Bye, honey.

———————

MISS FAYDA MAE'S FRUIT COCKTAIL
GRAVY COBBLER

1 large can fruit cocktail
¼ cup light brown sugar
2 tsp cornstarch
1 can Mandarin oranges

3 Tbs margarine
1 cup Bisquick or the
   likes
½ cup cream

With the syrup from the drained fruit, mix the light brown sugar and cornstarch. Stir over fire till thick. Add the fruit and bring to a boil. Empty into a square baking dish and smear on 2 tablespoons of the margarine. Mix Bisquick, cream and the rest of the margarine (it should be moist but stiff) then spoon over the hot fruit cocktail. In a 400-degree oven cook for 20 minutes. The biscuits should be golden.
Serves 6.

AUNT BIMMIE'S MEAT AND BEANS

2 lbs ham hocks with a
   lot of meat or
   chopped ham
2 lbs dried big lima
   beans
6 cups water
2 onions, chopped

½ cup diced celery
2 Tbs ketchup
1 tsp molasses
1 tsp French's mustard
1 tsp salt
   Black pepper to taste

Pick your beans good. Put them in a big pot of water and bring to a rolling boil. Turn off the fire and let sit for one and a half hours. Add everything else, cover and slow cook for 2 hours. Take the meat off the bones. Cook a pot of rice and chop a fresh bowl of onions to go with them.
Serves 6.

ROSETTA'S SPANISH POTATO CROQUETTES

6 medium potatoes,
  boiled
3 Tbs buttermilk
1 Tbs margarine
1 egg, beaten

1 Tbs minced onion
1 Tbs minced green
  pepper
1½ tsp salt
¼ tsp pepper

Whip the potatoes and all the above together. Pour out into a 2 inch deep pan and chill. Then form into croquettes (like little 2 or 3 inch high pones).

4 cups saltine crumbs
3 eggs (slightly beaten)

Roll the croquettes in the crumbs, then in the eggs and back in the crumbs. Deep fry in fat till golden brown and done through (2 or 3 minutes). Put on paper to drain. Delicious cold.
  Serves 6.

EGGS IN INDIAN GRAVY

9 hard-boiled eggs,
  chopped
8 Tbs chopped onions
5 Tbs margarine
4 Tbs flour
7 tsp curry powder

3 cups sweet milk
½ cup water
2 tsp salt
⅛ tsp pepper
3 cups of cooked rice

Cook the onions in the margarine. Take off the fire and stir in the flour and the curry powder. Put back on the fire and heat till smooth. Slowly pour on the milk and water while stirring until it thickens. Add eggs, salt and pepper. Pour over rice in casserole, cover and take it out the door cause there's hungry people waiting on you.
  Serves 4.

DEVILED PECAN EGGS

8 hard-boiled eggs
1 tsp French's mustard
1 tsp grated onion
½ tsp salt

1 tsp vinegar
¼ cup mayonnaise
½ cup pecans, chopped

With a sharp knife, half the eggs long ways. Remove yellows and fork till mashed. Mix in all the other ingredients and stuff back in the eggs. Arrange on platter. Don't forget to tape your name to the bottom of the dish.

LUCILLE COLLINS' DEVILED FISH EGGS

8 hard-boiled eggs
4 Tbs margarine,
   softened
3 tsp of them little black
   fish eggs

2 tsp vinegar
1 tsp sugar
⅛ tsp black pepper

Cut eggs the long way. Take out yolks and mash with fork. Then mix with sugar, margarine, vinegar and black pepper until very smooth. Fold in the fish eggs and stuff the whites with the mixture. Sprinkle with paprika.

"She brings 'em cause they go good with beer," Gracie says.

GRACIE'S SUGAR COOKIES

2 cups sifted flour	1 egg
1½ tsp baking powder	⅔ cup Crisco
¼ tsp salt	¾ cup sugar
4 tsp milk	½ tsp vanilla

Sift together the dry things. Cut the sugar into the Crisco and add the vanilla. Beat in egg till fluffy. Add milk and stir till smooth. Slowly blend in the dry mixture. When creamy store in the icebox till chilled. Roll out on a floured spot until an eighth inch thick. Cut in circles and bake for 10 minutes at 350 degrees on an ungreased sheet. Remove from pan and cool.

Makes 22 to 26 cookies.

LEFTOVER COFFEE DESSERT

6½ cups very strong hot coffee	1 cup light brown sugar
3 packs Knox gelatin	1 tsp minced crystallized ginger
½ cup cold water	¾ cup toasted chopped Brazil nuts
2 sticks cinnamon	
4 cloves	

Cook the coffee for 10 minutes on a slow fire with the cinnamon and the cloves in it. Fish out the cloves and the cinnamon. Soften the gelatin in the water. Add it and the sugar to the hot liquid and stir until it dissolves. Chill in the icebox. When it starts to set and thickens fold in the ginger and the Brazil nuts. Chill until very firm. Tear into hunks and place in a bowl with whipped cream. If you want, add a little Irish Mist to the cream.

CORN PUDDIN

2½ cups fresh cut corn
    kernels
2 eggs, beaten
1 cup milk
¼ cup finely chopped
    celery
¼ cup finely chopped
    onion
1 stick margarine
2 Tbs flour
1 tsp salt
½ cup Ritz cracker
    crumbs

With the margarine in a cast-iron skillet, cook the celery and the onions till soft. Blend the flour and the salt to the mixture. When it begins to bubble slowly pour in the milk, constantly stirring. While rapidly stirring, bring to a rolling boil and stir and cook for 2 or 3 minutes more. Add the cut corn and stir in the beaten eggs. Pour into a greased baking dish. Cover with Ritz cracker crumbs and cook in the oven at 350 degrees until firm or a toothpick comes out clean. Serves 6.

CHESTINE BUTLER'S MEAT LOAF

2 lbs ground meat
½ tsp salt
½ tsp black pepper
1 cup celery, chopped
2 Tbs Worcestershire
    sauce
1 can tomato soup
1 tsp baking powder
3 eggs, well beaten
1 onion, chopped
1 green pepper, chopped
2 cups hard bread,
    crumbled
½ cup ketchup

Work everything into the ground meat except the ketchup. You've got to use your hands. When blended, put in a greased glass baking dish and cover with the ketchup. Bake at 375 degrees for one hour being careful not to let it burn.

Chestine slices it and makes cold sandwiches with mayonnaise and mustard. Serves 6.

CLAUDETTE CAHILL'S BOILED AND BAKED HAM

Whole ham (pre-
cooked)
1 cup brown sugar
2 Tbs French's mustard
6 cloves

Cold beer
Water
1 jar Maraschino
cherries, cut in half

Cut off some of the fat. Crisscross ham, making diamond-shaped cuts. Boil in the sugar, mustard, cloves and enough beer and water to cover. When tender (an hour) drain. Put on baking pan and place cherries in all the diamonds. Then pour cherry juice over it and brown in the oven at 400 degrees for 15 or 20 minutes.

Claudette says, "You can take a ham anywhere."

REATHA FAYE'S SQUASH RITZ CASSEROLE

1 lb yellow squash, cut
in rounds
½ cup crumbled Ritz (23)
1 onion, chopped
½ cup celery, chopped
fine
½ cup grated sharp
Cheddar cheese

¼ cup green pepper,
chopped fine
2 eggs beaten
1 cup sweet milk
½ cup evaporated milk
¼ tsp salt
2 Tbs melted margarine
Pepper

Tenderize squash in a little bit of water, drain and mash. Mix all the other ingredients in with the squash. Butter a casserole and put the squash mixture in it. Bake at 350 degrees for 30 minutes or so. When done it should be kind of like a pudding.

Serves 6.

AUNT SUTIE'S COMFORT BANANA PUDDIN

First, The Scratch Puddin:

5 eggs	1 cup sugar
1½ cups sweet milk	1 Tbs flour
1 cup evaporated milk	Pinch or two of salt
1 Tbs vanilla	

If you ain't got one, rig up a double boiler by putting another pot inside a bigger pot with water in it and put it on the fire.

Pour the milk into the heated pot. Mix together and add, very slowly, the sugar, flour and the salt to the milk, stirring constantly. Don't stop stirring. Cook for about 20 minutes more after it has started to get thick. Reserve egg whites in a clean bowl, and in another bowl beat the yolks. Stir a spoonful or two of the pudding into the yolks and mix thoroughly. Then add it all to the pudding and stir up very good. Stir and cook for 5 more minutes, take off fire and fold in the vanilla. Now that's your scratch puddin.

Comfort Crust:
Vanilla wafers
7 ripe bananas, sliced in rounds

In a baking dish make a layer of wafers and a layer of bananas, then pour on a layer of the puddin. Keep doing this until all the puddin is gone, but remember you must wind up with a layer of puddin.

The Meringue:
5 egg whites
½ cup of sugar
1 pinch of cream of tartar

Beat whites till peaked. Then add the sugar, a little at the time, and beat until peaks curl over and hold. Spread the meringue over the pudding and put it in a 425-degree preheated oven for 6 or 7 minutes. Careful not to let it get too brown. By the time you get to the wake or wherever you're going it will be set up good. It's also very good chilled.

AUNT MELVILLE'S OKRA AND TOMATOES

1 lb okra, sliced
1 can tomatoes
   Onions

Lots of hot stuff
(Tabasco sauce,
Worcestershire sauce,
peppers)

Tump it all together and simmer 2 or 3 hours.
   This'll perk 'em up.

SUE ETHEL'S SAUSAGES AND BEANS

1 lb hot pork sausage,
   loose
2 cans red kidney beans
2 cans stewed tomatoes
2 cups tomato juice
2 or 3 bay leaves
1 large onion, chopped
1½ tsp seasoned salt

½ tsp garlic salt
1 tsp chili powder
½ tsp thyme
¼ tsp black pepper
1 cup whole kernel corn
2 stalks celery, chopped
1 green pepper, chopped

Brown onions, sausage, celery, and green pepper. Add everything
else, cover and simmer for one hour.

WILLARD LYNN'S LIMAS WITH A TWANG

3 cups cooked dried lima
   beans
½ can stewed tomatoes
¼ cup finely chopped
   onions
2 Tbs brown sugar

1 tsp vinegar
1 tsp Worcestershire
   sauce
1 tsp French's mustard
4 slices bacon

Put your beans in a 2-quart baking dish. Mix mustard, Worcestershire sauce, vinegar, tomatoes, brown sugar, onions and 2 slices of diced bacon. Put over beans. Cut bacon into four pieces and lay on top. Bake in a 375-degree oven for 45 minutes to an hour.
   Serves 4.

JEWELDEEN'S DEVILED-CRAB EGGS

12 hard-boiled eggs
½ cups mayonnaise
1 small can crab meat,
   drained and flaked

3 Tbs finely chopped
   onion
1 tsp French's mustard
   Salt and black pepper
   to taste

Lengthwise cut the eggs in half and remove the yolks. Mash them up and mix well with the mayo, onion, mustard, salt, and pepper. Stir in the flaked crab meat and then fill the eggs back up. Chill. Garnish eggs with a tiny sprig of parsley. Don't load it down if you're takin 'em to a wake.

MRS. TOOLER DOOLUS' OVEN SPAGHETTI

1 lb ground meat	1 can stewed crushed
2 green peppers, sliced	tomatoes
1 medium onion,	1 can ripe olives, no pits
chopped	Salt and black pepper
2 Tbs vegetable oil (only	to taste
if you need it)	12 oz spaghetti, cooked
2 eggs, beaten	½ cup Ritz cracker
2 cups corn kernels	crumbs
	Oleo

Fry the ground meat until brown. Add the green peppers, the onions and the oil (if you need it) and cook until limp. Take off the fire and add the eggs. Then the corn, tomatoes, and olive and mix well. Add to the spaghetti and pour into a big baking dish. Sprinkle on the cracker crumbs and pat with oleo. In a 375-degree oven, bake for 40 minutes.

"With a loaf of lite bread, this'll feed the multitudes," Mrs. Doolus said.

Serves 6.

HOMALENE'S SOMBRERO BEAN DISH

1 lb ground sausage	1 large can pintos
1 can tomato sauce	1 medium bag of Doritos
1 can Old El Paso	¾ cup white cheese,
Enchilada Sauce	grated
2 green peppers,	
medium to hot	

In a deep skillet cook sausage until it crumbles up real good but not brown. Add everything to the skillet in layers. Reserve some corn chips and cheese for the top. In a 350-degree oven bake covered for 30 minutes. Uncover for the last 10 or until top is crispy and brown.

She says you can eat 'em with your hat on.

FELICIA BATTEN'S SWEET FRIED PIES

2 cups sifted self-rising flour	1 egg yolk
¼ tsp baking powder	¼ cup sugar
1 tsp salt	½ cup evaporated milk
2 Tbs Crisco	Canned fruit (apples, peaches or pears)

Into the flour, baking powder and salt cut in the Crisco. Mix egg yolk, milk and sugar then add to the flour mixture. With a rolling pin roll out to a quarter inch on a floured surface. Cut in 4-inch squares. Spoon on a little bit of fruit, remembering that you are going to fold them point to point, so they'll come out like triangles. Fold over the fruit and seal the edges with a fork. Repeat till all dough is gone. Fry in a skillet with about an inch of very hot shortening until brown.

You have to watch the ladies with these. They go easily into their pocketbooks for later. Delicious with a glass of milk.

BILLIE RONDA'S FAMOUS BOURBON FRANKS

½ cup good bourbon whiskey	3 tsp dark brown sugar
½ cup tomato ketchup	1 lb frankfurters
	Toothpicks

Stir together bourbon, ketchup, and sugar in a pan set over low heat. Now put the heat up, but don't let it boil. Cut franks into bite-size pieces and add. Stir a bit, cover the pot, and let sit on the back of the stove overnight. Next day, when you've got folks coming, just heat it up again without it bubbling. Then you've got yourself something—just make sure you've got toothpicks and a load of napkins for the drips. Toothpick 'em. Put on tray and surround with saltines. Some at the wake will just want to nibble!

Enough for a crowd!

GRAMMA DORA'S FRIED CHICKEN

1 medium fryer, cut up
1 quart buttermilk
2 cups flour
1 Tbs baking powder

1 tsp paprika
Salt and pepper
3 cups Crisco

Pour the buttermilk over the chicken and soak for a few hours. Drain off the buttermilk. Pat chicken pieces into the flour, salt, pepper, baking powder, and paprika. Heat Crisco in deep iron skillet and fry. Turn frequently to get that crispy brown. Takes about 25 to 30 minutes.

BIG RUBY DUKES'S PEACHADILLIES

1 package fluffy white
   frosting mix
1 cup flour
⅓ cup cooking oil

1 cup peach preserves
¼ tsp cinnamon
1 cup finely chopped
   almonds

Prepare frosting mix as directed on the package. To half of the frosting mix, add flour and oil. Pat into bottom of a greased 13 x 9-inch pan. Bake at 350 degrees for 10 minutes. Spread with preserves. Fold cinnamon and almonds into the remaining frosting and spread over preserves. Bake 25 to 30 minutes longer or until topping is golden brown. Cool slightly. Cut into bars.
   Makes 36 bars.

NETTY BLOCK'S SALMON CROQUETTES

1 tall can salmon
4 tsp margarine or oleo
¼ cup all-purpose flour
½ cup evaporated milk
1 Tbs lemon juice
1 Tbs finely chopped
  onion

Salt and pepper to taste
1 cup fine crumbs
  (saltines crumbled)
1 beaten egg
2 Tbs sweet milk
1 package frozen green
  peas in white sauce

Drain off the juice from the salmon and save a half cup. Get rid of all the skin and bones while flaking the meat. Melt oleo and stir in the flour. To this add your salmon juice and milk. Cook until thick, stirring constantly. Add lemon juice, onion, salt and pepper. Mix in salmon and put in the icebox till cold. Form into 8 balls, roll in crumbs and make cones. Dip in beaten egg and milk then back in crumbs. Fry in deep hot fat till brown, 2 to 3 minutes. Drain on paper towels. Fix peas by package directions and top each croquette.

Serves 4.

CANDY SILCOX'S CONFETTI EGGS

6 hard-boiled eggs
2 tsp finely chopped
  toasted almonds
2 Tbs minced green
  pepper
1½ tsp minced pimiento
1 Tbs chopped ripe
  olives

3 Tbs Hellman's
  mayonnaise
1 tsp salt
1 tsp vinegar
¼ tsp black pepper
  Dash hot pepper sauce

Cut eggs in half long ways. Take out the yolks and mash with a fork. Mix everything with the yolks and stuff the eggs.

Because of the color these might not be appreciated at some wakes.

ANY OCCASION PIMIENTO CHEESE SANDWICHES

1 5½-oz can evaporated
   milk
½ lb processed American
   cheese, diced

1 3-oz can pimientos
¼ tsp salt

Combine milk and diced cheese in the top of a double boiler and heat until cheese melts. Drain pimientos and mash. Add to the melted cheese, along with salt.

Makes enough for 8 sandwiches. But cut 'em up in quarters and they go a long way.

YELLOW-EYED DEVILED EGGS

1 dozen fresh yard eggs
   (boiled)
2 tsp mustard
1 Tbs mayonnaise

2 tsp sweet pickle relish
1 tsp minced onions
Salt and pepper
Paprika

Slice eggs in half, reserve and mash yolks. Blend in the mustard and mayonnaise. Add pickle relish, onion, salt and pepper. Stuff the egg whites with the yolk mixture and lightly sprinkle with paprika.

NAIREEN THE PERLOW QUEEN'S SAUSAGE PERLOW

2 lbs smoked sausage
½ cup onion, chopped
¼ cup celery, chopped
2 Tbs bell pepper, chopped
1 piece garlic, chopped
1 regular can stewed tomatoes
1 tomato can of water

1 fist of thyme (the coarse kind)
3 bay leaves
2 hot green peppers or Tabasco to taste
Salt and black pepper
2 cups rice, Uncle Ben's
4 cups water

In a good heavy perlow pot, fry sausage, onions, celery, bell pepper and garlic till brown. Add tomatoes and the one can of water. Bring to boil, add thyme, bay leaves, hot pepper, salt and pepper to taste. Cook down for 20 to 25 minutes. Add rice and water and bring back up to a boil. Put tight lid on and simmer for 45 minutes, stirring once about half way through. If it's too soggy take the lid off for a while. If it's too dry add a bit more water.

"That Naireen is sumpthin. She's at the door with her pot, 'fore you can say perlow," Gracie said.

OVEN BROCCOLI

1 stick margarine
1 large onion, chopped
1 small can mushrooms
1 box frozen broccoli

8 oz cheese, chunked
1 can cream of mushroom soup
1 cup Uncle Ben's rice, raw

Fry onions in margarine till tender. Drain and add the mushrooms, then the broccoli, salt and pepper to taste. Cook until tender, about 15 minutes. Mix the cheese and mushroom soup together and add to what's already in the frying pan. Cook the rice in two and a half cups water, and add it. Pour it all into a casserole and bake for half an hour at 325 degrees or for 10 minutes in a microwave. Bread crumbs and Parmesan cheese may be put on top before baking.

LUCILLE COLLINS' WHISKEY PIE

Crust:
1½ cups graham crackers,
    crushed
¼ lb butter, melted
⅓ cup sugar
Dash cinnamon

Filling:
12 oz cream cheese
½ cup sugar
2 eggs, beaten whole
1 Tbs flour
3 Tbs whiskey

Topping:
1 cup sour cream
3 Tbs sugar
1 Tbs whiskey

Make a kind of dough mixing all the crust ingredients together and press them into a pie pan, covering bottom and sides. Soften cream cheese, beat altogether with flour, sugar, eggs, and whiskey until thick as cream. Pour into the graham cracker shell. Bake at 375 degrees for 20 minutes. Mix the topping ingredients and spread on pie and bake 5 minutes more. Chill.

Lucille says, "This is strickly for wakes."

FAMILY REUNIONS,
BARBEQUES,
FISH FRYS,
AND PICNICS

POLLYS & MOLLYS

In Bacon County, Georgia, there's a town called Coffee. And in that town there's a chapter of the U. D. C. that, at one time, sported the largest number of surviving daughters of a Confederate soldier anywhere in the South, or, for that matter the world. The Captain Ovid Osteen Newberry Chapter of the United Daughters of the Confederacy had this organization sewn up on the local, state and national level. Now, they weren't moneyed (in fact, they were land-poor), but no one would have ever known it by the way some of them kept up the proud, proud front. There was Fannie Newberry Perry, Annie Newberry Walters Potter Floyd (Fannie said, "She keppa marryin 'um an they jus kept own a dyin"), Ovella Newberry Drake, Carrie Newberry Wooten, Molly Newberry Vanups, and Polly Newberry Vanups. The two youngest, Polly and Molly, married sophisticated Charleston railroad men and moved up and away in the world, never, again, to let on that their family didn't have two dimes to rub together. However, by rights, they did have the most money of all the girls, but it was, to no means, a fortune. They could afford to buy a fur, a fancy hat and a diamond. They both drove big, long black cars, too, especially, when they went to see their Bacon County country sisters.

Ovella said, "They jus tryin to keep up with them Charleston women who've got diamond rings big enough ta eat dinner on and more than ample blue rinse in their hair to color the Satilla River all the way to Woodbine." So, it seems, when you've come from a little country town and have lived in Charleston your entire married life with all those Van Dasterpoops, as Ovella calls them, you can't imagine how far down the road Coffee, Georgia must have seemed. Still, the only reason they had been accepted into Charleston society, at all, was because of their connection with the world's largest chapter of the U. D. C. in the South, even if it was in Bacon County, Georgia. And that was the ONLY reason. Now that was prestige to them Charleston folks. The sisters couldn't talk enough about their daddy, Ovid Newberry Newberry Newberry Newberry, otherwise they would have been considered South Georgia trash—

which they were from time to time. However, most of their children had heard it all too many times and couldn't wait to get back down in the swamps and scrubs of South Georgia and North Florida just to escape what they called "the Charleston Blue Bloods." The Newberry name had gotten Molly and Polly out of the woods and into town, but their children couldn't return to the swamps and scrubs fast enough.

Big Polly had a daughter and named her Molly Newberry Vanups. Big Molly had a daughter and named her Polly Newberry Vanups. Both of the daughters married brothers from a questionable Cracker family of the Georgia-Florida border area. Questionable by Charleston standards, anyway. So now, there was Floyd and Polly Newberry Vanups Bevels, Lloyd and Molly Newberry Vanups Bevels. And the two of them had had umpteen children, too, who were all just as ladened with names, like walking family trees. But Floyd and Lloyd ignored all of it. They didn't care who was named what. So, it was left, totally, up to the women to keep it going. And they did. Sometimes without catching a breath.

It was the six sisters, four of them that had populated ever dirt road in Bacon County and the two that had tried to get their toehold in Charleston society. They were ALL obsessed by the Newberry name. And as time went on Big Polly and Big Molly, after losing their husbands, started feeling the guilt of having neglected the Vanups's name. All they had ever thought about was the Newberrys, because it was their ticket. They had Newberryed their children up the wall and right under the noses of all those Charleston Vanupses, too. So now in their old age they wanted to do something about this neglect, while they still could. And it was such a perfect and convenient time to make amends. The Charleston Gazette had just run a big article on the Vanupses, letting everybody know from Savannah to Myrtle Beach that there was to be a big Vanups family gathering in the form of a barbeque, fish fry picnic. The paper requested the presence of everyone bearing the Vanups's name and anyone else directly related 'by blood' of course. The Gazette also advised the families to bring their own special covered dish to be shared on one big common table with everyone, but the barbeque and the fish would be furnished. It said it was to take place at the

Vanups State Park on Bunters Island right outside of Beaufort. Big Molly and Big Polly were thrilled about the coming event. They figured that it was their chance to uphold the Vanups's name and, after all these years, to redeem themselves, just a little bit. They believed, at their age, each one of these gatherings might be their last. So, they both sent out the article to all their children and made the decree that not only were they all expected to go to the reunion but they would also congregate at their respective mothers' homes (next door to each other) on Gardenia Lane and that they would all drive the sixty-some-odd miles from Charleston in a caravan, procession style. Both Big Molly and Big Polly feigned close to the grave illnesses to make sure Polly and Molly and their broods would come all the way from Florida.

On the day of the reunion, it was obvious from the sheer numbers that the decrees and faked sinking spells had worked to rally the family together one more time as only a Southern mumma can do. Both of the houses were filled with great-great-grandchildren right on up to the sons and daughters. And the cars were lined up on the street ready to begin the pilgrimage to the Vanups Family Reunion. When they had packed them with food of every description known to the South and equal numbers of children, all ages, the caravan slowly pulled out onto the highway. Big Molly and Big Polly in the first car, with one of their oldest sons driving and one riding shotgun, began to reminisce about their late husbands, Russ and Gus, as they passed through Rantowles, and about how Molly and Polly had been born while on a railroad expedition down into North Florida and how they've lived there ever since. While they passed Garden Corners, they talked about the christening when Big Molly stood for Big Polly's Molly and Big Polly stood for Big Molly's Polly. And that Molly and Polly were as devoted to each other as Polly and Molly had been down the years. Two sisters with two daughters, each as the other's namesake. This to them was the way to keep their families double-connected. However, not long ago at a Newberry Reunion, Ovella was ostracized after having said, "I bet you a crook to a dog's tail neither Big Polly or Big Molly, if you ask 'em point blank, couldn't tell you if they was married to Russ or Gus an whether it was Molly or Polly that's er daughter. I ain't

even shore they know which 'un of 'ems which 'un, let alone, remember whether they was married to Floyd or Lloyd. They don't
know Pollys from Mollys, anymore. It's a mess."

The chain of cars curled its way along the marshes into Beaufort
and again the memories of Gus and Russ came pouring out. Or was
it Russ and Gus. Then somewhere around Frogmore they both realized that, now, the reunion was scarcely over the bridge and waiting for them. They were just plain excited about the entire family
making an appearance at the outing and thought not much else
mattered to them, now. It was a time to show off all their family to
whoever might have showed up from Charleston. And, after all, it
had always been a numbers game with them.

As the car carrying Big Molly and Big Polly entered the gate of
the park, they could vaguely see a slough of people up ahead.
While fidgeting with their thick, thick glasses, and pushing and
shaping their hair with a pat of the hand and a pick of the finger,
they readied themselves for whatever was to come, knowing that
their near blindness could be pulled out of the hat, and used, if it
got to the point of not recognizing or remembering. When the
Russ and Gus Vanupses' caravan was in full view of the crowd, every
head under the big pavilion shed turned. Just as every eye in the
procession focused in on, what looked every bit like, two separate
reunions. One at each end of the large covered picnic area. This
was obvious even to Molly and Polly, though they claimed seeing
nothing else. They figured that it must be two different church
groups having their own service to begin the reunion. At this point
no one had ever owned up to the truth that the Charleston Vanupses
were split in more ways than religious ones. And this publicly announced gathering was the end all at providing them with a reunion most would never recover from. Molly and Polly included.

Big Molly and Big Polly worked their way over with the help
of the sons to the first crowd of people they could get to and began
introducing and asking how each one belonged. They were strain-
ing ever so hard to see and recognize what they could. But not
being able to see much and hearing even less, the sisters just started
in. "Dahlin, how good to see you. Ouuh, you got that jet black
hair just like my Polly." "Oh I haven't seen you in years, but that
voice. It sounds just like Gus's Mumma." "Dahlin, look at you.

You got a tan as dark as my Molly. How's yo Mumma?" "I'd recognize you anywhere with that big toothy smile. You've got to belong to Vic and Clarice's bunch." "Them eyes, honey, you look just like Gus's daddy. There's no hidin that." The lack of response from the group didn't faze them as they went on and on, but the rest of the family stuck close to their cars in shock, not believing what they were seeing and, even less, what Big Molly and Big Polly were saying and doing. They resisted every attempt by the sons to guide them away from that crowd to the other end of the pavilion and went on greeting, kissing and recognizing. Little Molly and Little Polly refused to get out of the car and, even more, refused to put their food on that common table. And it was obvious now that there were two common tables in the making.

Big Molly and Big Polly's families had started trickling down to the other end of the shed and the place was buzzing. One of the uppity, old-line Vanupses, took it on herself, that she would go and get the "two old Jawga sisters," before they disgraced the family beyond repair, and, especially, before the newspaper reporter got there to take pictures of the picnic, even if she had to drag them back by the hair of the head. But she simply told them that it was communion time and she knew they didn't want to miss that. They recognized her, for real, and followed her like sheeps to the other end, just in time for the passing of the communion wafer by the priest. Kneeling, they took the wafer and said Amen. Then came the deacon with the wine chalice. Big Molly and Big Polly started fumbling in their pocketbooks for something. At the very same time they both came out with a fist full of pennies, nickels, dimes and quarters and dumped them right in the communion wine. While everyone bit their tongues, the priest and the deacon, completely bewildered, fished out (pocketed) the money and continued the rounds.

After the service the sisters were told of the mixup in the reunion and that they had been down at the other end, hugging and kissing a bunch of Negroes who happened to have the same last name and showed up for the wrong reunion. Simultaneously Big Molly and Big Polly gasped, "Ooooh, go own now!!" Their daughters jumped on them for disgracing their family in front of all those Charleston relatives. And the relatives were just as upset and had begun to lash out at them with their big Charleston mouths. But it hit Big Molly wrong. Her mind had slowed, but by no means was it gone, and like an old rusty Bacon County 'bobwire' fence that had been stretched and pulled for fifty years, it snapped. She took Big Polly's hand, clasped it and began in a loud, but dignified, voice, "First of all, I don't know what the hell y'all are so upset about, they everyone lighter than the whole bunch of you. And I distinkly remember hearing your granddaddy say, years ago, 'You may not like all the Vanupses but you GOT to love 'em. Defend 'em to the death.' So I think you all better sit down and have some of this food that everybody's brought and have a real good communion. And if that ain't enough, I got to tell you that even with these feeble ol eyes, I cain see they all look just like you."

She unclasped Polly's hand and said to her, low-like, "Now I don't nesairly believe in all this, but we cain't ack like animals. We just got to make the best of the sitchiation." Big Polly was quick to give her support and said, "Let's grab a plate and get to THEIR table for some good food. I'm thirty-years tired of Anna Belle Vanups's fancy Charleston Turnip Souffle. This'll almost be like goin home to Coffee." Big Molly said, "Lawd, I hope to Gawd the United Daughters don't get wind of this."

BIG MOLLY'S CHERRY COBBLER

4 cups canned pie
    cherries (No pits!)
¼ cups quick tapioca
1 pinch of ground cloves
¼ tsp cinnamon
1 pinch of salt

1 cup of light brown
    sugar
1 Tbs of grated orange
    rind
2 cups of Bisquick

In a great big pan mix the dry stuff (but not the Bisquick) and stir together with the pie cherries. Bring it up to a boil and cook for five minutes. Oleo down a two-quart baking dish and pour the cooked mixture in it. Make your Bisquick like it says on the box and spoon it on top of the cherries. Put it in the oven at 400 degrees for 20 to 25 minutes. Until the Bisquick is good and brown.

Serves 4 or more.

PICNIC TARTAR SAUCE

1 cup Hellmann's
    mayonnaise
¼ cup dill pickle relish

1 tsp grated onion
1 Tbs chopped canned
    pimiento

Stir together and put in the icebox to chill or take the stuff and make it when you get there.

Makes a bit more than a cup.

UNCLE BUBBA'S BARBEQUED RIBS

5 lbs meaty spareribs
½ cup ketchup
1 tsp brown sugar
1 tsp Worcestershire
   sauce

1 tsp vinegar
2 squirts of Tabasco
2 Tbs French's mustard
Salt and black pepper
   to taste

Grill the ribs over medium hot coals (hickory chips) until tender (two hours or so). Make sure you turn them a lot so as they don't burn. Mix up all your sauce ingredients and heat it so it will blend together. When the ribs are done spread the sauce over them and continue cooking for 20 or 25 minutes more. You can also bake them in a 300-degree oven for one and a half hours or until ribs are tender. Don't forget to turn the ribs once so they'll brown on both sides. Brush with the barbeque sauce as they bake.

Serves 6.

REUNION RICE PUDDIN

1 can crushed pineapple
2 Tbs white sugar
1 cup quick cook rice
1 cup water
½ tsp salt

1 Tbs lemon juice
1 banana, chopped
1 medium bag miniature
   marshmallows
1 cup whipping cream,
   whipped

In a saucepan mix up the rice, water, syrup (from the drained pineapple), sugar and salt, and stir enough to moisten the rice. Cook to a quick boil, turn down heat, cover, and simmer 5 minutes. Set off the heat and let stand for 5 minutes. Now pour in the lemon juice, pineapple, banana, and marshmallows. Let it cool and fold in the whipped cream and eat.

Will serve 8, but better for 4.

SASSY'S HUMMINGBIRD CAKE

3 cups all-purpose flour	1 8-oz can crushed
2 cups sugar	pineapple, undrained
1 tsp salt	1½ tsp vanilla
1 tsp cinnamon	¾ cup chopped pecans
1 tsp baking soda	¼ cup black walnuts
1¼ cups cooking oil	⅔ cup mashed bananas
3 eggs, well beaten	

Combine all the dry ingredients in a large bowl. Add eggs and oil and stir until ingredients are moistened. *Do not use electric mixer.* Stir in vanilla, pineapple, nuts, and bananas. Spoon batter into three 9-inch round cake pans that have been well greased and floured. Bake for 25 to 30 minutes at 350 degrees. Cool 10 minutes, then turn out on cake rack to cool completely. Then frost.

Hummingbird Frosting: cream together two 8-oz packages of cream cheese and one cup softened butter. Blend in two 16-oz packages confectioners sugar. Add two teaspoons vanilla and one cup chopped pecans and mix thoroughly.

It's so sweet you can feed an army of hummingbirds.

OVELLA'S BEEFED-UP PORK AND BEANS

1 lb hamburger	⅓ cup brown sugar
1 large onion, cut up	3 Tbs French's mustard
1 quart can of any pork and beans	Bacon, enough to cover top
1 can tomato soup	Salt and pepper to taste

In a deep cast iron skillet brown the hamburger and the onion. Then drain off the grease and the juice. Add everything else to it and put the bacon on top. It'll take one hour in a 350-degree oven and it's ready.

Serves 6.

POLLY'S BEDEVILED CRABS

2 cups of fresh crab meat (canned will do)	1 dash of red hot sauce
8 Tbs margarine or butter	1 pinch of dill
1 Tbs flour	½ tsp salt
1 Tbs lemon juice, fresh squeezed	1 cup buttermilk
1 Tbs French's mustard	1 little sweet bell pepper, chopped fine
2 Tbs ketchup	1 little onion, chopped fine
2 tsp Worcestershire sauce	3 hard-boiled eggs, chopped
	½ cup bread crumbs

In a saucepan melt 4 tablespoons of margarine and slowly add flour, stirring till smooth. Put in the next seven things and pour on the milk, slow like, and cook over low fire till thick. Put a cover on it and set it aside. In a skillet fry the onion and pepper in about a spoon more of the margarine until they are soft. Combine with sauce and then add the egg and the crab meat. Press into tinfoil crab shells and pat on the buttered bread crumbs (buttered with the rest of the margarine). Bake in a hot 425-degree oven for 10 minutes. Make sure they are good and golden on the top.

Serves 6.

POLLY'S PUPPY HUSH-UPS

1¾ cups self-rising corn-meal	1 egg
1¼ cups buttermilk	1 tsp salt
1 small onion, chopped	2 tsp sugar
	8 Tbs drippings

Mix up the meal, sugar, and salt. Add the buttermilk and the beaten egg and stir till just right. Combine with onion. Heat up the drippings until they sizzle and crack, then add to the batter and stir fast. Plop by tablespoons in hot fat and fry till crispy brown. You might have to turn them if your fat is not deep enough. Don't overload the frying pan. When done, drain on paper.

Serve with fried fish, grits and cole slaw.

Will make 20 to 25 hush-ups.

EDNA MAE'S SLAWDOWN COLE SLAW

1 head cabbage	Some salt
Some sugar	Sweet pickle juice

Shred cabbage. Sprinkle sugar and salt onto cabbage and squeeze into cabbage with your fingers. Slaw should "weep". Add sweet pickle juice, seeds and all.

Sometimes you might have to turn your head so it'll cry.

HUMBLE LOG CABBAGE STEW

1 lb ground beef	1 16-oz can kidney beans
1 onion, sliced thin	1 cup canned tomatoes
1 cup cabbage, shredded	1 tsp salt
½ cup celery, diced	Dash pepper

Brown up the beef, then throw in the onions, cabbage, and celery. Cook until yellowish, then add two cups water and simmer for around 15 minutes. Slip in the rest of the ingredients and continue cooking for 15 to 20 minutes. And to give Mrs. Lincoln's stew a continental look, serve it on top of mashed potatoes. The two cups water may not be necessary, as there is plenty of juice in the canned beans and tomatoes.

AUNT BELLE'S CHARLESTON PEANUT BUTTER LOGS

1 cup crunchy style
   peanut butter
1 cup powdered sugar

3 Tbs soft butter
2 cups Rice Krispies

Mix all these ingredients together and roll into small logs. Dip in frosting.

Frosting:

1 cup powdered sugar
3 tsp milk
Vanilla

After dipping in frosting, roll logs in melted chocolate, graham cracker crumbs, or coconut. Set in a cool place, if they last that long.

FREDDIE LOU'S GEECHEED CABBAGE

4 slices bacon, cut up
⅓ cup finely chopped bell
   peppers
4 Tbs onions, chopped
1 can stewed tomatoes
1 tsp sugar

1 tsp salt
1 tsp French's mustard
   Dash of pepper sauce
6 cups chopped cabbage,
   cooked

In a big heavy pot fry bacon, green peppers, and onion until crisp. Add everything else and stir in good. Cook until heated through. Put on rice for the best and only way to get Geechee flavor.

Makes 4 to 6 servings.

AUNT CALIOPE'S MIXED-UP BEANS

12 slices of bacon, cut in
    squares
1 medium onion,
    chopped
1 lb of chopped ham
½ cup dark brown sugar
½ cup ketchup
2 tsp French's mustard

1 tsp salt
1 can baby green limas,
    drained
1 can Boston style baked
    beans
1 can red kidneys,
    drained

Fry and drain bacon in skillet. Brown onion in drippings and take out. Pour out drippings and brown ham. Drain off fat. Mix all else together and put in a three-quart baking tin or dish, cover and cook in slow oven (300 degrees) about an hour.

Makes 6 to 8 servings.

GRANNY'S REVISED TEA CAKES

2 sticks butter (soft but
    not melted)
2 eggs

1 cup white sugar
4 cups self-rising flour
1 tsp vanilla

Cream the sugar and butter. Beat the eggs and add to the butter-sugar stuff. Mix thoroughly and pour on the vanilla. Sift the flour and combine with other. Mix well. Chill dough in the icebox until it is firm and you can roll it out. Roll it thin and cut to desired shapes. Bake in a 350-degree oven until golden on the top.

Makes about 4 dozen cookies.

MRS STAFFORD'S CAROLINA POUND CAKE

2 sticks butter	1 Tbs lemon
½ cup Crisco	1 tsp vanilla
3¾ cups flour	3 cups sugar
1 cup milk	1 tsp salt
5 eggs	

Cream together the butter and Crisco and sugar. Add milk and blend. Add eggs one at a time alternating with about a cup of the flour at a time, beating after each addition. Add salt. Add the lemon and the vanilla and blend. Bake in tube pan at 350 degrees for one hour and 15 minutes.

WAVY FLAG CAKE

1 package white cake mix	4 eggs
1 13-oz package strawberry gelatin	½ cup water
	¾ cup oil
2 Tbs flour	1 10-oz box frozen sliced strawberries

Mix cake mix, gelatin, flour, eggs and water. Beat at medium speed for two minutes. Add thawed strawberries, including syrup to the batter and beat one minute. Add the oil and beat one more minute. Pour into greased 13 × 9 inch pan and bake at 350 degrees for 40 minutes. Cool 10 minutes, then turn out onto platter. Frost.

Frosting:

1 cup whipping cream, beaten until stiff	Fresh blueberries
¼ cups powdered sugar	Fresh strawberries

Mix whipping cream and powdered sugar and frost cake. Stick the upper left hand corner with 50 blueberries and arrange fresh strawberries in stripes, against strips of cream between. Refrigerate.

KATHERINE BELLE'S APPLE CAKE

1½ cups cooking oil
2 cups sugar
3 well beaten eggs
3 cups raw, peeled, and
    diced apples

1 cup chopped pecans
3 cups flour
1 tsp soda
2 tsp vanilla

Combine the oil, sugar, eggs, apples and pecans in a large bowl. In a separate bowl sift the flour and soda. Add this to the apple mixture. Stir well with two teaspoons vanilla. Bake cake in 3 large layer pans at 325 degrees about 35 minutes.

Frosting/filling:
1½ sticks oleo
1 box light brown sugar
⅔ cup canned condensed
    milk

2 tsp vanilla
Grated coconut

Cook oleo, brown sugar, and condensed milk altogether over low heat. Let it come to full boil. Beat till cool, not cold, adding vanilla. Spread and sprinkle coconut between layers and on top.

ANNA BELLE'S FUDGE PIE

2 squares of bitter
    chocolate
1 stick of butter
2 eggs

1 cup sugar
1 cup flour
1 tsp vanilla

Melt chocolate and butter, add vanilla. Mix flour and sugar. Beat eggs and combine with flour mixture. Add chocolate mixture and mix well. Pour into a well greased pie pan. Bake at 350 degrees for 30 to 40 minutes. Will cut like a pie. Serve with whipped cream or ice cream. You double this recipe for a bigger pie.

GRANDMA'S POUND CAKE

2½ cups sifted self-rising
    flour
1½ cups sugar
¾ cups milk

1 cup shortening
½ cup butter
5 fresh yard eggs
1 tsp vanilla

Beat mixture for 20 minutes. Bake 350 degrees for one hour.
You won't believe the difference them fresh eggs'll give you.

BIG POLLY'S CRACKER CAKE

32 saltine crackers
2 cups sugar
1½ tsp baking powder
2 cups pecans
6 egg whites
1 tsp cream of tartar

1 8-oz carton Cool Whip
1 8-oz can crushed
  pineapple, well
  drained
Frozen grated coconut
Candied cherries

Use a rolling pin to crush the crackers until very fine. Mix them together with one cup of the sugar, the baking powder and pecans. Beat the egg whites until soft peaks form, add cream of tartar and the rest of the sugar and continue beating until stiff. Fold the mixture of dry ingredients into the egg whites. Pour into a well greased pan and bake at 350 degrees for 25 minutes or until golden brown. Watch closely. Remove cake carefully from pan after cooling. Chill. Frost with Cool Whip. Spread top with pineapple and cover with coconut, then garnish with cherries. The cherries are for when you need something extra fancy. Or you can frost it with Seven Minute Frosting and garnish with just cherries and pecan halves.

SEVEN MINUTE FROSTING

2 egg whites
1½ cup sugar
1½ tsp light corn syrup or
    ¼ tsp cream of tartar

⅓ cup water
Dash salt
1 tsp vanilla flavoring

Place all ingredients except vanilla flavoring in double boiler. Mix thoroughly. Cook over water beating constantly with rotary or electric beater until mixture forms peaks, about 7 minutes. Remove from heat. Add flavoring. Beat until spreading consistency.

BIG MOLLY'S CRACKER PIE

3 eggs
1 cup sugar
1 tsp baking powder

12 saltines
12 dates
¾ cup pecans

Beat eggs. Add sugar and baking powder. Crumble saltines into this. Let stand. Cut up dates and add. Add pecans. Pour into buttered pie pan. Bake 350 degrees for 35 minutes. Serve plain or with whipped cream.

AUNT FANNY'S FISHFRIED OYSTERS

1 quart of big fresh
  shucked oysters (no
  coon oysters for this),
  drained
2 eggs, beaten

¼ cup Pet evaporated
  milk
  Salt and black pepper
1½ cups of cracker meal
  (crumble saltines real
  fine if you can't find
  cracker meal)

With a fork beat the eggs, milk, salt and pepper together. Drag each oyster through the batter then turn it in the cracker meal till it's covered. When you've got enough, put them in hot grease one at a time. Fry three minutes or until golden. Don't overcook your oysters. If they are small you can stick two or three together with the batter and then roll in the meal. You can also take this right to the picnic ground and fry them there.
  Serves 6.

HOLIDAYS
AND
SUCH

CHRISTMAS SHOPPIN

Jerry Dale Holly was sowgded down in an old front porch rocker, mesmerized by the shooshing of a mile of pine trees that surrounded the house. In chilly weather the porch belonged to him and he used it to do his thinking, especially, while he made out his gift list for the coming Holidays. However, when Jerry Dale was younger he hid up-under the porch, listened to the grown-ups go on and on about everybody's presents, caught flicked cigarette butts to make smoking chimneys on little sand houses for Sanny Claws to come down, and chummed up doodle bugs out of their caniving holes for Juanita's main Christmas present. He was positive, his older sister by two years, just loved doodle bugs. Certainly, she always screamed loud enough.

Now, at thirteen, the rocker in a state of dilapidation is his place to chum and conjure a whole headful of catalogues, fancy department stores and wish books for his mind to go shopping in. He sits for hours. Stupefied. And for hours Mumma, Glennie Nell, hollers, "Jerry Daaaale. . . . . Jerry Daaaale. Me and yer sister cain't do all this Christmas cookin by areselves. Git . . . in . . . here, else you ain't gone git a mouth of it when it's done." Next time she'd holler, "Jerry Daaaale. . . . . Jerry Daaaale. . . . . git in here 'fore I slap you right off that front porch all the way to Biloxi." "Jerry Dale ain't heard nothin, Mumma. He's too busy shoppin for Christmas presents," Juanita said. "In his mine, you mean," Mumma snipped. But Jerry was deep, deep in thought, on what he could buy for Juanita now that she'd lost her taste for doodle bugs.

While Glennie Nell cooked, she seemed to harp continuously, in her head, at Jerald Dale Sr. about how she believed that Juanita was titched, at least Christmaswise, by them doodle bug presents. Because now, she wanted the craziest damn things every year. The kids could see her lips moving, to herself, as she went on reminding him, still in her head, of course, that at thirteen, Juanita asked for a statchers head of somebody named Bay Toe Vin, and last year she wanted a packige of some things called Papa Domes "cause they jump up outta the grease at ya when you try n fry 'em." That youn'un, what in the name o gawd will she wont nex? Mumma thought. She had already got a feeling, and she told Jerald Dale Sr. too, that, whatever it was, channel thirteen on the TV set was just as to blame for her lack of good sense as was Jerry Dale's doodle bugs. At least, when it come to choosing Christmas presents. Just recently she, couldn't stand it any longer and had to confess to one of her social club members, "We cain't git her out of that ol Chinese housecoat that she found in a box of things Jerald Dale brought back home from the War."

Jerry Dale used his big ears, each year, to be the first to find out what Juanita wanted. So, with his one or two trips to town at the most, he'd desperately try to find it himself. Then, if he couldn't, he'd tell his mother and father, just to watch them roll their eyes. But he was always set off by Juanita's pick and spent about all of his time and money trying to find it. Especially, since the sum-total he ever bought his Mumma was, Evening in Paris, talcum powder, or a lace handkerchief with a big GNH on it. She claimed that's all she ever wanted. His daddy was even less exciting to buy for; shaving foam, or Old Spice.

Juanita had decided long ago what she wanted, but so far she didn't let on to a soul. Not even Jerry Dale. But now might be the time to tell him and get him in off that front porch before Mumma's threats become real, she thought. She knew Jerry Dale would scramble for the kitchen at just one mention of the word present. So, it was her thinking that if she'd let them both know now, what she wanted for Christmas, it might also save Jerry Dale a trip, right off that front porch, to Biloxi.

Jerry Dale flew into the kitchen and paused at the edge of the table which he gripped with his fingers. Mumma folded her arms, tilted her head and looked over her glasses at Juanita. "Y'all wont laugh at me, will ya?" Juanita begged. Mumma said, "Honey, I might cry, but I'll never laugh at what YOU want for Christmas." Jerry Dale stood still and silent with his ears tweeked. As quick as her lips could get it out Juanita blurted, "Madame Butterfly." Jerry Dale didn't change a hair, but, with the queerest look, of absolute flabbergastation the child had ever seen, Mumma eyeballed Juanita and said, "Madum Budder Whooooo?" "Madame Butterfly," Juanita repeated. Mumma went back to stirring the cake batter, squenched up her nose real bad, and said, "Now . . . jis . . . whut, own the back of white cat's ass, is that?" Jerry Dale gripped the table even tighter, hoping Juanita would come up with a good explanation. Juanita began, "It's stowry-music." "Why who sings it, honey," Mumma, trying to keep calm, fished, "Dolly Parton? An if she didn't, I betcha she wrote it." "No, Mumma, it comes from a long time ago in It'ly. A man by the name of P-U-C-C-I-N-I wrote it," Juanita pleaded. "Well, I cain't even say that, let alone know what the hell kinda stowry is it. Nex thing ya know we gone need a interpruhtater ta tawk t' ya," she said with her over-worked nerves. "Weeeeell, it's about love," Juanita said. "Love! I mighten ta knew it," Mumma said with more irritation than ever, "I bet it's jis full a necked people, ain't it?" "Naooooo, it don't have necked people in it, it ain't that kinda love," Juanita said now, with a little more nerve of her own. But she quickly decided to get on and tell the whole story, while she could.

"It's about a soldier, looooongtime ago, that falls in love with one of them Japanese women and marries er while he was stationed over there. But he gits sent home and has ta leave er. He swears to er he'll be back as soon as he can." Mumma can't stand it and breaks in, "I've heard all that before." "Now, Mumma, let me finish 'fore you say another thing," Juanita, trying not to lose her place, picks up again, "But, you wrong, cause he does come back. Only thing is he brings an American wife with im." "I coulda told you that too, honey," Mumma assures her. Juanita tries to ignore her and goes on, "But the Japanese woman is so hurt n upset by it all till she commits suicide.". . . . . "That's it!! That's damnedest song I ever heard of. She oughten to a shot that son-of-a-bitch right in it. I tell ya, sometimes, I swear they all alike. . . . . But, honey, them mixed things jis ain't never worked, any ways. That's proof-puddin. Even, that ol Italian knew it." "Oh Mumma," Juanita shrugs, "that's not what the stowry means. It's a sad, sad romance that ends even sadder. . . . . "Ta Je-e-sus Cramminy!! And you want that for Christmas?" Mumma gripes. "Yes I do! It's the music that makes it so pretty," Juanita rested. Mumma said, "Huuuh!!"

Jerry Dale had hung to every word that his ears heard and had already, at least mentally, gone shopping. He knew his only hope was the local record store. If they didn't have such a thing, Mrs. Rachel might could order it for him, even if it took every penny he had. Mumma would go on and git Juanita whatever she wanted to anyway and he knew it wouldn't be "Madame Butterfly".

It took Mumma a good three weeks, with the help of the children, to stir and bake and cook-up one of her fine Christmas dinners. And each year when she started worrying, out loud, about cooking too much food, tight mouthed Jerald Dale Sr. would up and say, "Don't worry bout it, Mumma. It'll get et." She knew that he was right, and said to herself, "Them ciddy relatives 'od descend on 'em like Japanese grasshoppers and eat like they ain't et since last year."

Well, Christmas day came and Juanita got her "Madame Butterfly" and everyone else got just what they wanted too. Juanita went straight over to the record player and put it on. It was Christmas, Mumma couldn't say a thing. But she couldn't stand it either, so, she finished putting the touches on her dinner and took to the yard. She did love seeing the city relatives each Christmas, even though she felt a slight bit taken advantage of, but she figured, it was Christmas, and she did love doing it.

They all arrived about an hour later. Three carloads. Mumma was sitting on the front steps, Jerry Dale was in one rocker and Jerald Dale Sr. was in the other. When the crowd, stacked with presents, reached Mumma, she stood up to greet them, shy like. Greetings was always so awkward, she thought. Then, someone missed Juanita and asked where she was? They could hear the opera playing in the background but couldn't figure it out. They had never heard such a thing as that in Glennie's house before. Then, Mumma throws up her hands and said, "She's in there listenin to Pooch-er-Neen-Neenie er somebody." That broke more than just the ice that year. They all laughed, even Mumma, and went on in the house for a good Christmas Dinner. As they sat down, Madame Butterfly was over in the corner dying. The usually silent Jerald Dale Sr. again spoke up, "Gaw-od dawg! Somebody give that calf some more rope." "Cramminy ta Jesus, Jerald Dale Holly Sr., not right here at the Christmas table," Mumma said, putting a quieatous on the whole thing.

GLENNIE'S GUINEA HEN BAKED

2 or more cleaned
   guineas
   Small slab of salt meat
8 or 9 slices of smoked bacon
1 cup of strong coffee
½ tsp of vinegar

1 tsp of sugar
Salt and pepper
3 rutabagas, cut in
   hunks
Butter, salt and pepper
   to taste

First thing: boil rutabagas until tender. Add butter, salt and pepper and set on the back burner.

Guineas: first off, guineas are hard to come by. Most likely you got to raise 'em or know someone that does. But if you can git 'em they worth every bite. A grown hen'll weigh two and a half to three pounds cleaned. So you can plan on 3 to 4 people to the guinea. Course if you got other things, like I always do, it'll go a longer ways. I fix two or three to please my Christmas crowd. It's dark meat an has a light gamey taste to it. That's what makes it different from chicken. In fact, I clean it just like a chicken. Then I stuff a piece of salt meat and some black pepper in the hole. Wrap it all up with the slices of bacon and tie it up with string, if you want. Stick 'em in a fry pan or Dutch oven just big enough to hold 'em and a little deep so you don't lose your juice. It's best if your oven is already at 350 degrees or maybe a little hotter and they'll be done in an hour give or take a few minutes. But if you want to brown the breast take off the bacon and put it back in the oven for another 10 or so minutes. When it's ready, cut up the meat on a hot platter, surround with rutabaga hunks and keep it warm. From the juice spoon out some of the excess fat. Put in the coffee, sugar and vinegar. Move pot to a high burner and cook till all the guinea goody is loose from the bottom and sides. Pour this, hot, over the cut up meat and rutabagas. Take it straight to the table.

Careful of them old guineas cause you can cook 'em all day and still cain't bite into 'em.

GLENNIE NELL'S ROAST CHRISTMAS POSSUM

1 live possum	5 or 6 slices of bacon
½ cup vinegar	Salt and pepper
Kitchen Bouquet	8 to 10 medium sweet potaters
Persimmon jam	

Now, Christmas possum is different from all other possum. It's got to be caught, not killed, two weeks to a month before the cookin day. That's right around late November. You can catch 'em in the hen house, or up a 'simmon tree or in a trap. It don't make no never mind, long as he's caught live, cause they got to be penned up so you can clean 'em out. Feed 'em nothin but corn bread and milk. That'll fix 'em up, fatten 'em out, and get rid of all them no-good flavors. This makes possum as good as corn-fed pig. Then, when the time comes, kill 'em quick, skin the rascal an git shed of all the insides.

Now you got a possum ready for cookin. Sink 'em in a 'namel dish pan or basin and make sure he's good an covered. Then add a half cup of vinegar and let it soak in the icebox overnight. In the morning drain off the water and cut up the possum into rabbit pieces. Thata way the city folk'll never know they eatin possum. An I'ma tellin ya it works. Boil the possum pieces in enough salted water until it's done, but not fallin off the bone. This timin depends on the age of the possum. Sometimes it's ready in a hour, other times it'll take two. When it's done, fish out the pieces and drain 'em. That'll git ridda just about all the possum grease. When it's cool, so you can handle it, rub the rabbit-size possum pieces with salt and black pepper. Plenty. Then make a mixture of Kitchen Bouquet and half a jar of persimmon jam. I always make my jam just after the first frost cause then it's sweeter, that is, if the possums ain't done et 'em all. Just a teaspoon or two of the Kitchen Bouquet and stir it into the jam. Now, if you ain't got persimmon jam, any light tastin one'll do. Smear the stuff all over the pieces until you've got 'em coated good. Lay on four or five slices of salt pork or bacon and surround it with ya greased sweet potaters. Put it in a hot oven at 350 degrees and roast, covered, for thirty min-

utes. Then uncover it and cook till it's sizzlin browned but never burned (about another thirty minutes). Spoon the juice up on it every few minutes while it's uncovered. I don't think I know a soul that don't surround their possum with sweet potaters, cause it takes just about a good hour for 'em to bake. Be extry shore ya possum is done. They ain't nothing in the world worst than bein accused of servin half-baked possum.

SHOULDER ROAST OF PORK

1 pork shoulder	½ cup brown sugar
Garlic	¼ cup of bourbon
Flour, enough to dust	whiskey
it good	4 or 5 dashes of
2 Tbs of Crisco	Worcestershire sauce
½ cup French's mustard	Salt and pepper

Take your fresh shoulder and rub it round with a little bit of mashed garlic (not too much cause it'll hide the taste of the pork). Do same with salt and pepper. Wrap it up and let it sit in the icebox at least two hours (all night's best). After that dust it all up with flour and fry it rich and brown on all sides in Crisco. Dutch oven's best for this. Put the mustard in a bowl with brown sugar and add the Worcestershire sauce and whiskey, stirrin. Mix and smear on the roast and put a lid on it. Tight. If you ain't got a tight pot, seal it in tinfoil. Bake in the oven at 200 degrees or 225 degrees for 6 hours or so. If you put it in the stove just before you go to bed Christmas Eve it'll be ready by mornin. With this you ain't got to worry about raw pork, plus it's juicy. All the work's done overnight. It's like havin a Sanny Claws helper.

MADAME BUDDER WHO'S OPRY FUDGE

2 cups sugar
1 cup evaporated milk
½ tsp salt
1 Tbs margarine
1 tsp vanilla

½ cup marshmallow
  creme
½ cup chopped candied
  cherries

Combine in a heavy saucepan the sugar, milk, and salt. Heat over medium heat, stirring constantly till sugar dissolves and mixture comes to a boil. Cook to soft ball stage, and stir only if you have to. Take off the fire, add margarine and cool to warm. Don't stir. Add vanilla and beat till it begins to hold its form. Mix in the marshmallow creme, beat till very thick and starts to get dull. Fold in the cherries very fast and spread it out in a big greased platter. Mark it off in squares while it's still soft and warm. Then cut when it hardens.

COOKED APPLES

5 large cookin apples
1 cup sugar
1 tsp cinnamon

¼ tsp nutmeg
¼ cup butter
2 Tbs water

Combine sugar, cinnamon, and nutmeg. Peel apples and cut into chunks. Sprinkle sugar over apples and mix thoroughly. Put seasoned apples, butter, and water into pot, cover, and cook over low heat, stirring once or twice, for 20 minutes or until apples are tender.

These can be as good as sweet potatoes when you serve 'em with the pork.

SWEET TATER PIE

1 cup mashed cooked sweet taters	½ tsp lemon extract
⅔ cup sugar	½ tsp cinnamon
2 eggs, beaten	½ tsp salt
1 cup evaporated milk	An unbaked pie crust

Scald the milk and mix everything together. Pour into the unbaked pie shell and bake at 425 degrees for 20 minutes, reduce to 350 degrees and continue another 20 or so minutes. Make sure the crust is good and brown. Cool before serving. It's best warm.

JUANITA'S PINEYWOODS HOT TAMALE

1 lb hamburger	1 regular can ripe pitted olives, chopped
1 onion, chopped	1 can cream of chicken soup
1 can hominy, drained	½ pint sour cream
1 can HOT tamales, chopped (make sure you dehusk 'em if they got 'em)	Salt and pepper

Brown the hamburger and onion with salt and pepper to taste. Add the hominy, tamales, olives, chicken soup and sour cream. Mix well and pour into a two-quart baking dish. Bake at 350 degrees for 30 minutes.

Juanita learned this in school during Around the World Week. Serves 6.

SOUTHERN SNOW BALL CAKE

1 large angel food cake	1 cup sugar
2 envelopes Knox gelatin	1 cup chopped pecans
¼ tsp salt	1 large can coconut
4 envelopes Dream Whip	1 can crushed pineapple, 1 lb 4 oz size

Cut cake in half, one half for bottom layer and the other half for top layer. Dissolve two envelopes of gelatin in two teaspoons of cold water. Add one cup boiling water, stir and let stand 10 minutes. Add pineapple, salt, sugar, and nuts, and put in icebox for one hour or until firm. Mix two envelopes of Dream Whip as directed on package. Fold into gelatin mixture. Break cake into small pieces and put in a 9 x 14-inch pan. Spread half the gelatin mixture over cake then do the same with the other half cake and mixture. Then mix the other two envelopes of Dream Whip and fold in half cup coconut and spread over the top and sprinkle with the rest of the coconut. Chill for a few hours.

AUNT DECKARD'S MINCEMEAT PIE

(With Real Meat)

6 cooking apples	¾ cup grape wine (Mogan David is good)
1 lb cooked roast beef	
1 cup dark raisins, packed down	1 tsp cinnamon
1½ cups sugar	1 tsp cloves

Stem, core (don't bother to peel) apples and slice thin. Then cut the apple slices into 8 to 10 pieces. Cut the cooked roast into small pieces about the same size as the apple pieces. Mix all ingredients (except spices—add them last) and let stand overnight or for a week in the refrigerator. Put in a pie crust, cover with top crust and bake 350 degrees for 45 minutes to a hour.

COUSIN PAT'S BIG SCRUB AMBROSIA

Add together in a bowl fresh oranges, grapefruit, coconut, and some canned pineapple—it helps cut the grapefruit if it happens to be on the tart side. Always serve in those green dishes, the ones you get for premiums at the gas station.

HOLIDAY ICEBOX CAKE

2 cups fresh cranberries, chopped
1 large banana, sliced
⅔ cup sugar
2 cups crushed vanilla wafers

½ cup butter
1 cup confectioners sugar
2 eggs
½ cup chopped pecans
1 9-oz size Cool Whip

Mix together cranberries, banana, and two thirds cup of sugar. Set aside. Place one half of the crushed vanilla wafers in bottom of buttered 8 x 8-inch glass pan. Cream butter and confectioners sugar together, add eggs and beat well. Spread this mixture over the crumbs. Now top with the cranberry mixture and sprinkle with the chopped nuts. Spread the Cool Whip over the cranberries and chopped nuts. Cover with the remaining crushed wafers, and chill at least 4 hours or overnight.

CRIMSON TIDE CHERRY SALAD

1 can sour pie cherries,
   drain and reserve
   juice
1 Tbs lemon juice
   Soda water
1 cup sugar
1 small envelope
   unflavored gelatin
2 Tbs cold water

1 6-oz package cherry
   Jello
1¾ cup soda water
1 cup sliced celery
1 cup sliced stuffed
   olives
1 small package cream
   cheese, make 13 balls

With cherry juice, add lemon juice and enough soda for two cups. Mix sugar and bring to a boil. Dissolve gelatin in cold water and stir into the heated mixture. Just add the cherry Jello straight to the hot liquid. Stir until dissolved. Mix one and three quarters cups soda water and chill until starts to get thick. Lightly stir in cherries, celery and olives. Pour into a greased mold. Poke down the balls of cheese here and there. Chill until firm and unmold.
   Makes one 7-cup mold.

AUNT WANNY'S CHRISTMAS RICE CREAM

1½ cups cooked rice
2 cups evaporated milk
6 egg yolks, beaten
1 cup sugar
   Pinch of salt
2 tsp almond extract

6 egg whites, beaten stiff
2 cans whole cranberry
   sauce
2 Tbs orange juice
½ cup light brown sugar

Heat milk and sugar. Stir in egg yolks and cook till starts to thicken. Add rice, salt and continue to cook. Stir constantly until again thick. Then set off the fire and cool to warm. Add extract and fold in the stiffly beaten egg whites. Pour into a buttered baking dish and bake at 350 degrees for 20 or so minutes or until firm and slightly browned on the top. Cool or chill and top with Sanny Claws Sauce.

Sanny Claws Sauce: heat cranberries, orange juice and sugar till all is dissolved. Pour over the Christmas Rice Cream when ready to serve. Serves 10.

SANNY CLAWS SALAD

3 envelopes Knox gelatin
1 cup sugar
1 cup light brown sugar
½ cup water
   Pinch or two of salt
1 cup celery, sliced thin
1 small grapefruit, peeled and sectioned

1 orange, peeled and sectioned
1 quart bag fresh cranberries, cleaned
1 cup pecans, chopped
1 8-oz can crushed pineapple

Grind together the cranberries, grapefruit and the orange. Add to the water and sugar and cook until dissolved. Add the gelatin and mix until dissolved. Add all else and mix. Pour into a Jello mold or flat pan and chill. Serve on lettuce leaves with a spoon of mayonnaise and a cherry on top.

PLAIN OLD GUINEA DRESSING

4 cups day-old corn bread, crumbled
1 sleeve coarse crumbled saltines
½ stick oleo
1 yellow onion, chopped

½ cup celery, chopped
1 tsp ground sage
½ tsp salt
½ tsp black pepper
½ tsp poultry seasoning
   Chicken juice

Mix crackers and corn bread together with everything except the juice and mix well. Pour juice, a little at a time, until moist but not soupy. Bake at 350 degrees until brown but not dry.

This is enough dressing to go with 2 or 3 baked guineas. Double it if you want more.

AUNT NAOMI'S BAKED HAM

1 15-lb ham, precooked
   Whole cloves
¼ cup pineapple/orange
   juice
1 Tbs cornstarch
¾ cup brown sugar

1 Tbs French's mustard
1 small can sliced
   pineapple
1 small jar Maraschino
   cherries

Cook ham in water. Drain. Take off all the fat except a thin layer.
Sit ham, fat side up, in a shallow baking dish. Cut diamond shapes
across the back of the ham and stick each with a piece of clove. Mix
juice, cornstarch, sugar, and mustard. Spread over ham. Place pineapple rings on ham and put a cherry in the middle of each hole.
Bake in a 250-degree oven until the glaze bubbles, about 30–40
minutes.
   This's also a MUST at Easter with potato salad and asparagus.

GREEN BEANS AND NEW POTATOES

3 lbs of fresh snapped
   and stringed green
   beans, any variety

2 lbs of new potatoes,
   little tiny ones
3 ham hocks

In a big pot of water (the amount you think would cover the beans)
boil down the ham hocks until they are tender. Add the potatoes
and beans and cook till tender. If you like your beans a little crispy
add them when the potatoes are almost done. Drain bean liquor
and save for corn bread eatin.

CHEYENNE PACETTI'S HOLIDAY FRUIT SALAD

Pineapple, chunks or crushed, in its own juice (put in first so apples don't turn brown)

Apples, cut in bite-size chunks
Pecans, pieces or halves
Cherries
Coconuts, shredded

Put it all in a bowl. Use your own amounts.

OLD MRS HOLLEY'S WHITE FRUITCAKE

4 cups shelled pecans
¾ lb candied cherries
1 lb candied pineapple
1¾ cups all-purpose flour
½ lb oleo

1 cup granulated sugar
5 large eggs
½ tsp baking powder
½ oz lemon extract
½ oz vanilla extract

Chop nuts and fruits into medium-size pieces. Dredge with a small amount of the flour, about a quarter cup. Cream oleo and sugar until light and fluffy. Add well beaten eggs and blend well. Sift remaining flour and baking powder together. Fold into eggs and oleo mixture. Add vanilla and lemon extracts. Mix well. Add fruits and nuts. Blend well. Grease a 10-inch tube pan or 2 loaf pans. Line with heavy brown paper and grease again. Pour batter into prepared pan or pans. Place in a cold oven and bake at 250 degrees for 3 hours for tube pan or 2 hours for 2 loaf pans. Cool in pan or pans on cake rack.

Makes 5 pounds.

HAWG
KILLINS

HAWG KILLIN ACCORDIN TO UNCA T.C.

Don't let nobody tell ya it's easy. But, when you get ready, you got to kill 'em quick. But, first, let me tell you about a little fishin trip. (Aunt Evie got up and left the front porch in disgust.) I loaded up my boat and old kicker in the back of my truck and took off for Pineywoods Island fish camp. You know, Aunt Erma Lee's boy, Sebert, runs it. I got there early and bought me some bait and he help me put my boat in the water. The tide was real low. I putted on out to Cabbage Creek and fished for two or three hours. Not a bite. So, I reeled in and started to head back to the camp. When I got back to where Little Pineywoods Creek empties into Big Cabbage Creek, what do you think I see? An ol sow with two young shoats swimmin right down the creek. I hadn't caught a fish er nothin, so I thought I might catch me a little pork. I hate to go home empty-handed. I wheeled the boat around and tried to head 'em off in the water. Cause I knew if they got to land, they was long gone. The sow and one shoat broke away an hit the bank, pourin the coal to it. But the other shoat went right out, smack dab, in the middle of the big creek and started a swimmin like he was headin for New York. I knew he couldn't make it, so I decided to go after him. When I did catch up with 'em, I reached down and grabbed an ear and a leg an threw 'em in my boat. Well, he almost beat the bottom out of it and just about made me jump overboard before I could get my hands on 'em and, what else but, hawg tie 'em. I made it back to the fish camp with him a flam-a-de-bamin the boat and pulled up to the dock where Sebert was standin. I looked up at 'em and said, "What the hell kinda bait did you sell me, Sebert? Look what I done caught." He look right back at me and, without as much as takin a breath, said, "You ol fool, you, it weren't the bait it's that number-three hook and slidin sinker. It'll catch 'em every time."

After four weeks of corn, acorns and a good hard frost, I butchered my catch of the day. An Mumma made a Pig Pickin Cake, 'specially for the occasion.

PIG PICKIN CAKE

1 box Duncan Hines
    yellow cake mix
1 can of Mandarin
    oranges, drained

1 package Jello Instant
    Vanilla Pudding
1 tub Cool Whip
1 can of crushed
    pineapple, drained

Mix up your cake like it says on the box. Stir in the drained orange pieces, put in a cake pan and bake. Dump pudding in Cool Whip and mix good. Fold in drained pineapple and refrigerate to cool before icing the cake.

But the first thing I do after the hawg's butchered is take the tail pieces down to Verna May to make us a Pigtail Perlow.

VERNA MAY'S PIGTAIL PERLOW

4 or 5 pigs' tails (you might
    want to chop 'em up
    but the kids like 'em
    whole)
1 large onion, chopped

Salt to taste
Black pepper to taste
1 pinch of sugar
1 to 2 cups of uncooked rice

Fry down your salted and peppered tails until they are good and brown. Add onions and do the same. When onions are brown, add enough water to cover. Simmer slow until the tails are tender. Add rice and bring to rolling boil. If the water doesn't cover the rice by a quarter inch, add more. Put a lid on your pot and turn the fire down to slow. Cook 15 minutes, check seasonin, and stir. If it's too dry, add a little more water. If it's too wet, put a tiny crack in the lid and it'll dry out some. This is one the kids love, cause they can have so much fun gettin the meat off the tail.

After I git that a-goin, I take to the other end and start on the head. And this is my favorite thing of the hawg killin. The Hawg's Head Cheese. They's as many different ways to make it as they is hawgs' heads, but I like it plain and simple like this:

HAWG'S HEAD CHEESE

1 hog's head
1 hog's tongue
Sage
Pinch of allspice
2 or 3 whole cloves

Chili pepper or red
  pepper
Vinegar
Salt and black pepper

Scrape and clean your hog's head, and trim and wash your tongue. In a big pot, cover with salty water, allspice and cloves and simmer until that meat leaves the bone. Drain and pick the head clean. Shred or grind all the meat including the tongue. I like to throw in a little bit of the ear gristle in mine. Season with the sage as strong as you like it and as hot as you want with the red pepper. Add a spoon or two of vinegar, salt and black pepper, and pack it in a bowl. Cover it and put a weight on it to mash out some of the fat and compress the meat. Some folks tie it up in cheesecloth and squeeze it. Either way works. Put it right in the icebox and let it stand for three days before you eat it. Then it'll slice up nice.

Now, that's it for the head and the tail. So, we'll go for the feet next. That's one of the tastiest parts on the hog. And they so easy. Most people just throw'em to the dawgs and don't bother with 'em, but not me. I fix 'em two different ways, dependin on my cravin. My first choice is pickled, cause I like 'em with a canna beer. But they also good, what they called, deviled. I think Miss Anna showed me how to fix 'em thata way years ago and she's kinda a fancy woman.

PICKLED PIG'S FEET

1 tsp whole cloves	1 large onion, sliced
4 bay leaves	1 hot green pepper,
4 cups white vinegar	whole
1 Tbs salt	Black pepper to taste
1 tsp sugar	

Take all four feet. Clean and scrap 'em till they spotless. Put in a pot and cover 'em with salted water and boil 'em until the meat is ready to come away from the bone. But don't let it. Don't forget to flip off the hoofs. In a pot go ahead and mix the vinegar, cloves, bay leaves, salt, sugar, onion, hot green pepper and black pepper. Cook to a boil for 20 or 30 minutes. Add 2 cups of the foot juice to the vinegar and stir. Put your feet in a jar so as they stand, if you can, and pour the vinegar over them. Cover and let 'em sit in the icebox for 3 days to a week. The longer the better.

MISS ANNA'S DEVILED PIG'S FEET

6 pig feet	1 tsp thyme
½ cup celery, chopped	3 bay leaves
2 medium onions, sliced	¼ tsp red pepper
1 carrot, diced	⅓ tsp of black pepper

I always ended up with 4 or 8 feet. I don't know how her recipe called for 6. I guess they threw 2 to the dogs. Anyway, put everything in a pot and cover with water. Simmer till tender, about 3 hours and a few minutes. Let the feet cool off in the pot. Then take out the loose bones from them and split long ways. Dowse in cornmeal and fry, or oven-broil till they are crispy and golden. I smear 'em with mustard and eat 'em. I think Anna just threw out that juice, but I season it up or down, whichever it needs, and I got me a soup.

We took care of the outside of the hawg, now we got to go inside. And the first thing that comes to my mind is the chittlins.

It's part of the intestines. So, you got to salt 'em and wash 'em and drain 'em, till they ain't no more water in the well. Then they clean enough to eat.

MAMA ELLEN'S FRIED CHITTLINS

Cut cleaned chittlins into small pieces and boil in salted water until tender. Drain off all the water. Salt, pepper and roll in cracker meal or cornmeal. Fry till golden and crispy.

Then you got what the old timers called hog lights. It ain't really no kinda light, it's the liver and the lungs. An it makes the best kinda stew. And with the liver you can make liver mush if you just want to make the stew outta the lungs.

HOG LIGHTS STEW

1 set of hog lights	Salt and black pepper
1 large onion, chopped	to taste
2 toes garlic, chopped	Flour

Chop your lights up into bite-size pieces. Fry down in heavy pot with the onion and the garlic till it is brown. Add water to cover, salt and pepper, and stew till tender. If it's not thick enough for you, use a little flour to make it thicker. Spoon that over rice and some Scratch Backs on the side, and you're fixed.

MUMMA PAT'S SCRATCH BACKS

This takes coarse ground cornmeal and a handful of cracklins. To the cornmeal and cracklins, add salt and enough boiling water to make it thick as putty. By hand, make small half inch thick pones. Fry till crispy and brown. Eat 'em hot slicked down with butter, if you got it. They so good and crunchy, they scratch your backbone goin down.

UNCA T.C.'S LIVER MUSH

1 hog liver, cut up, washed and picked clean of the membranes	Salt
	Black pepper
	1 Tbs thyme
¾ cups coarse ground cornmeal	1 Tbs sage
	1 tsp flake red pepper

Cook liver in salted water until tender. Drain and mash to a paste. Make a sluice of the liver and one cup of the liver juice. Put in pot and bring up to a boil while adding the cornmeal, till it gits good and thick. Add seasonings. Scrape into a mold of some kind and let it get cold. Remove and slice. It's a meal in one.

For the most part, everything else is just one cut of meat or another. Shoulders, hams, chops, ribs and bacon meat. Then, after that, the rest you fry down to render your lard. And that's where you git the cracklins. But, sometimes, I git a wild hair and I'll make the whole damn thing in sausage and it's done with. But I'll give it to you for a small batch.

MISS ANNA'S HOMEMADE SAUSAGE

2 lbs fresh lean pork	½ tsp allspice
¼ lb fat	1 tsp black pepper
½ tsp thyme	1½ tsp salt
1½ tsp sage	1 tsp vinegar
½ tsp celery seed	

Grind up the meat and the fat together. Add the spices and mix with your hands. You can make patties or stuff it.

What I like to do with this is make me a big pan of Dirty Rice. My brother raised coon dogs in Louisiana and he told me how to do this.

UNCA CLARENCE'S DIRTY RICE

1 lb fresh loose sausage
½ lb cooked hogs liver or
    any kind
2 large onions, chopped

3 toes garlic, squashed
Cayenne to taste
Salt
2 cups rice

Fry the sausage, onion and garlic till brown. Add crumbled up hogs liver. Season and put in the rice. Add water to cover and boil for one or two minutes. Turn down the fire and simmer until the rice is dry.

After all this smellin-up of the kitchen, cooking heads, feet and chittlins, you couldn'ta sleeped if Mama hadn'ta come and cooked a batch of Pickled Up Peaches and some Butter And Bread Pickles. This sweetened the house right back. And I can tell you word for word how she did it. (Aunt Evie came to the screen door, puckered her lip and left again.)

AUNT EVIE'S PICKLED PEACHES

18–20 small to medium
    peeled peaches
¼ cup whole cloves

2 cups vinegar
4½ cups sugar
3 cinnamon sticks

Boil the sugar, cinnamon, vinegar, and cloves for 15 minutes. Save enough cloves to stick two or three in each peach. Then drop peaches a little bit at a time into the mixture and cook them till they are tender but not overcooked. Put peaches in hot-scalded jars and fill with the peach juice. Make sure that every jar gits a few cloves and a stick of cinnamon.

Three to four quarts depending on the size of the peaches.

AUNT EVON'S BUTTER AND BREAD PICKLES

4 quarts medium cucumbers, sliced.	3 cloves garlic, chopped
6 medium white onions, sliced	⅓ cup coarse salt
	5 cups sugar
2 sweet green peppers, chopped	3 cups cider vinegar
	1½ tsp turmeric
	1½ tsp celery seed

Bring your sugar, vinegar, turmeric, and celery seed to a boil. Drop in everything else and bring back to a small boil (don't boil heavy), then jar 'em in scalded jars and seal them.

AUNT WANNY'S WATERMELON PRESERVES

1 lb watermelon rind	2 cups sugar
Water	½ lemon
2 Tbs lime (calcium oxide)	

Trim off outer green skin and pink flesh, using only greenish white parts of rind. Cut rind into one-inch cubes, and weigh. Dissolve the lime in two quarts water. Soak cubes for three and a half hours in lime water. Drain and place cubes in clear water for an hour. Again, drain off water and boil one and a half hours in fresh water, then drain. Make a syrup of two cups of sugar and one quart water. Add rind and boil one hour. As syrup thickens, add half a lemon, thinly sliced. When the syrup begins to thicken and the melon is clear, the preserves are ready. Pack them into hot sterilized jars, add enough syrup to cover, and seal.

While mama was doin this I'd git me a half a water glass of my latest homemade grape or berry wine and ease myself right on down into the evenin. You know, they weren't no such thing as TV back then.

UNCA T.C.'S HOMEMADE WINE

(Doubles Good)

3 pints grapes or berries
3 lbs sugar

Rinse and mash fruit. Mix sugar with enough water to dissolve it and add grapes or berries. Finish off a one gallon jar almost to the top with cold water. Cap it loose like and let stand for about 6 weeks. Strain, re-bottle, and stash it. It's best in a cool place in the summer.

SEWIN,
QUILTIN,
TACKY AND HOME
DEMONSTRATION
PARTIES

COVINA'S CLUTCH

Everyone showed up on Mrs. Covina Wright's front porch at the same time. The ladies, ever so slightly, elbowed each other, gently nudging, to get to her door. They were all anxious and twitching to show off their favorite prepared dishes that teetered in one hand, while a treasured bag of quilting scraps was clutched tight in the other. And there wasn't one of them that didn't have a giant pocketbook hooked in the crook of her arm. With everybody carrying handbags, scrap bags and casseroles, it was right crowded on the porch and a fidgety mess. After all, it was a day that the members of the Two Egg Quilting and Public Speaking Club waited for each week. Since, they all looked up to Covina, impressing her was of the utmost importance. She was the widow of the local undertaker and had been a comforting hostess at the funeral parlor until her husband died. Before that, she was a very well thought of schoolteacher. However, above all else that fascinated them with Covina was, they knew she had a little money. So, when the quilting was held at her house the girls always tried to do their very best.

Mrs. Wright was waiting for the group in her parlor. She heard the noise on the porch and hurried to open the front door before any of them could take a vote on "who would knock". It was too late. They had all knocked at the same time. When she opened the door the ladies had already lodged themselves in it. Covina's mind pictured a flock of guinea hens, all trying to get through the same hole in a fence. Then, her face went blank as she gazed out into the 'maylange' of hats and frocks from the Diana Shop swooshing against each other. Pocketbooks and shoes from Becks tapped and clicked together with a clink-a-dee-clank, that came, from what must have been a foot tub of Sarah Coventry jewelry. Mrs. Wright felt sure someone had dumped it on them as they came up the sidewalk and it stuck at random. But on top of all this was the cloud of Avon. Every scent ever produced. Covina's nose, particularly, twicked on the ancient smell of Tabu, "so old it had gone off," she thought. Then, out of the stacks of casserole dishes, pie plates, cake pans and mounds of tinfoil-covered things, came the scrumptious smell of food. It dominated everything and reminded Covina of the main reason for having a quilting party. Eating. The ladies always, nonchalantly, rushed through the business to get to the eating part of the meeting, even Covina.

May Ben Robbins broke the door jam first. She busted loose and headed straight for the kitchen, squealing, while in route, "mine's got to be put on the bottom rack of the oven, cause the top rack's too hot." "Mine goes up nex ta the broiler. It's got ta be browned real good," piped another. "Move out of my way, I got to get to the icebox, if you don't mind," sassily demanded another. And it went on and on until Beulah Harris, a foot taller than anybody there, and wearing what appeared to the ladies as men's clothes, spoke up and said, "I don't care where you put mine, but you better take it NOW, 'fore I put it some place you ain't gone want it." Beulah made a loud laugh and that ended it. She loved agitating the prissier ones. At once, they scattered and regrouped again in the quilting room and without hesitation started pulling on their wads of scraps. Every member of the club had her own handmade bag, personally sewn from some sort of tapestry or other fine material, which she used to carry her precious remnants. And, weekly, each tried to out-do the other by bringing the most beautiful or outlandish piece of fabric that could be found. While the others were digging, Beulah eased her large swath of black-and-white velvet print out of her paper sack. Covina spied the piece from across the room. She went directly to Beulah and, with her fingers rubbing the textured flocked velvet, she said, "This is it. The very piece we need to go on and finish our patterin." The other ladies didn't have a chance to look up, before Covina announced it was all over, like a queen making a decree. The group clucked with contempt, but knew Mrs. Covina Wright, with all that money, had taste and must be right. So, they went along with it. In five minutes the chosen piece was cut into about seventeen smaller ones (they loved hacking it up) and the sewing had begun. Covina was quick to remind them that the quilt must be finished today, since it was to be a wedding present, this coming week, for the daughter of the local preacher. The girls sewed with a little resentment in each stitch, mainly because Beulah's material was chosen. They were also hungry and no one really liked the preacher's daughter to

begin with. It was Covina's 'idear' to give the quilt to the new bride
but they still didn't like her. Anyway, they were sewing so hard no
one paid a bit of attention to the design on the outrageous fabric.
Beulah worked as quickly as the others knowing that, shortly, the
quilt would be finished, folded, put in a box and wrapped. Soon,
she would be as tickled as any to have that old scrap of hers domi-
nating the top of the preacher's daughter's quilt.

It wasn't long before Covina cleared her throat and in her re-
fined girls' school voice, as mistress of ceremony, said that it was
time for the two speakers of the week to share their talk about a
recent experience with the rest of the club. She quickly reminded
Willadoll Roundtree Peaster and Beulah Harris that the speech was
to be short, to the point, and directed at the members. They drew
needles. Beulah got the longest one, so Willadoll was picked to go
first. Reluctantly, she stood up by her place at the quilting frame
and made a kind of goat sound, then hesitated. Mrs. Wright immediately said, while thinking about the food in the kitchen,
"Come on, Willadoll, cat got your tongue?"

In a voice a little above a whisper and looking straight down
she said, "I's down to Williston the other day at a restrent where
my sister waits on tables." Covina interrupts, "Miseres Peaster,
don't talk to the quilt now." Willie didn't like it but looked up and
went on, "She tol me that Lacy Blodgett was rushed ta the Williston Hospital in so bad a shape they couldn't mov'er else she'd a
died. My sister said, them doctors down there cut her open an took
out er heart. Put it on a plane an flew it to Arlanduh in a beer
cooler. They fixed that thing an flew it back while Lacy laid up
there half dead, waitin for her heart to come back from Disney
World. She said, they put it in an sewed er up 'fore the plane'od lef
the groun. She's walkin all over Williston now jes like nuthin ever
hap'emed. It ain't no tellin what them doctors is a libel to do nex."
As Willadoll sat down, each lady turned to the next and mumbled
something so low nobody else could hear it. But for Covina, there
was no one to tell what she wanted. So she said, not knowing what
else to say, "My, that was a very intristing story, Willadoll. Thank
you very much."

Beulah was already nervous because she knew that Mrs. Wright
didn't waste any time between talks and she was next. "Well, Beu-

lah, it's your turn," she said, while thinking what kind of incredible story will I hear from this one. Beulah didn't wait a second, she stood up, gazed out the window and began, "Las week I took it on myself to find me a restin place. A cemetery plot. Y'all knowed I los my husban in a fishin accident and they never found 'is body so, I ownly need a place for me to be buried. I checked the newspaper and the television ads to see who had a nice cheap lot. But they was, all, too fancy or too expensive. On that, I called Wee Jean Watters," as she looks at her sitting down on the other end of the quilting frame. "I thought she might know of a place for me in my price range. I knew that her husban had sold cemetery plots, at one time, while he was in between jobs. So, she was the one to call. Well, Wee Jean said she knew just the place to look, but it was way up on the north end of the county. Now, knowing Wee Jean like I do, I knowed she'd tell ya just about anything ta git to go for a ride. But, I picked'er up anyways and we headed out. We was nearly to Jawga when we came upon this little hill that had a scatterin of scrub oaks on it. And I could tell by the look on her face that this was the spot. It had a hogwire fence and cattlegap gate, with a big wooden sign that said, COUNTRYLAWN CEMETERY. It was nuthin. An ol cow pasture. But Wee Jean kep at me till I got out of the car and walked round. I had to to shut'er up. She didn't say two words the whole time, but when we got back to the car she asked me if I liked it. So, I just lit in. Wee Jean, I said, I'd ruther be drug out on a hill and let the buzzards eat me than to be buried there. I've been shit on all my life and I ain't about to pay and be shit on by no bunch of cows forever after." Beulah sat down, laughing.

At first, no one could figure out whether she was finished or just quit in the middle, but Covina quickly seized the moment, in order to save the ladies from embarrassment. She offhandedly thanked Beulah and hurried on with the meeting. "The quilt is finished and ready to wrap. Please, don't anyone forget to sign the card. We want everyone to know who did all the hard work," she said. Each signed it and, one by one, scrambled for the kitchen to get their casseroles out of the oven. It was chaos, for a few minutes, with a hot dish in every hand and no place to put them. Then,

Covina came in and arranged the vegetables together, the meats with the meats, and all the sweet things in a row. They were simply amazed at how she could organize and how everything fell into place, for her. With that, they all gathered together, now feeling a closeness as they stood in line, ready to heap their plates. Even Covina.

When the time came round that next week for a meetin, everything had changed. The quilting club had broken up—and Mrs. Wright had disappeared.

You see, Covina generously offered to take the present to the shower for the ladies. And she did, right up to the front of the room. The preacher's daughter quickly tore off the pretty paper and ripped opened the box. The quilt was neatly folded and had the card on top. She picked it up and read all the names of the ladies aloud and thanked Mrs. Wright for all of them, since they weren't there. She grabbed the quilt and shook it out on a large, wide table where the shower-goers could see it. A quilt from the club was a prestigious gift in these parts. The ladies were famous for their handwork and their food. So, they were all filing by, to get a gander at it, when three of the staunchest and hardest shelled members of the Mount Olive Baptist Church went weak-kneed and started screaming. They dabbed and comforted themselves with kleenexes, little balled-up pieces of paper and handkerchiefs, while exclaiming what had dissolved them to this state. One hollered, "My Gawd, only the Devil himself would do it! It's filthy!" Another shrieked, "The hands of those women are the hands of Beasabub! I knew it all the time!" And the one dabbing the most with the kleenex said, "It looks ta me like a can of necked worms . . . doin it! Oh . . . my . . . Gawd!" The preacher's daughter didn't move. She stood there with a blank look on her face and still couldn't see what they were all carrying on about. Cautiously, Covina peeped over their shoulders to see exactly what had set off the hysteria. There, right on top of the quilt, was that black-and-white piece of flocked velvet, clearly, depicting a Roman Orgy. How she could have missed seeing it she didn't know, but there was no mistake. It was in bold print. Without considering anything, which was next to impossible for Covina, she made a dash for her coat and gloves, and was gone before anyone could miss her. At home, she threw some things into her suitcase and left, on a sudden vacation, with one thing on her mind. Beulah Harris.

And, to this day, Beulah swears that she didn't know a "thiiiing about it."

MAY BEN ROBBIN'S ORIENTAL OVEN PERLOW

1½ cups uncooked rice
2 Tbs margarine
½ cup onions, sliced thin
¾ cup celery, sliced thin
1 large green pepper, cut in long strips
1 can bamboo sprouts, drained
1 can water chestnuts, drained

3 chicken bouillon cubes, any kind
3 cups of water
3 Tbs soy sauce
1½ tsp salt
½ tsp pepper
1¼ cups almonds, slivered

Melt margarine in a pot and cook onions until limp. Add everything else but the rice and nuts and cook till hot but don't let it boil. Put the rice in a dry black iron skillet and toast it on top of the stove, stirring often. Put browned rice in a baking dish big enough to hold everything and pour the liquid on the rice and add the almonds to the top. Put on a tight lid and bake at 350 degrees for 50 minutes or until the liquid is all gone. If too dry add a little more water.

May Ben promises you: they'll think you've been to China. Serves 6.

MISS DICYS RICHMAN'S RICE

1¾ cups cooked rice
1 cup grated cheese
¾ cup chopped parshly

2 Tbs chopped onion
3 eggs
Salt and pepper

Mix the rice, cheese, parshly, onion, egg yolks (savin aside the whites) and salt and pepper. Beat whites till stiff and stir into the rice. Turn into a greased one-quart baking dish and cook at 350 degrees for 25 minutes. Serve it while it's hot.
Serves 4.

QUICK LORETTA

1 unbaked pie shell
10 slices of bacon, fried
   crisp
1 cup grated white
   cheese
4 eggs

2 cups evaporated milk
½ onion, chopped
½ green bell pepper,
   chopped
Small jar of pimientos

Crumble the bacon in the bottom of the pie crust. Sprinkle with grated cheese. Mix the other ingredients together and pour over the pie. Bake for 35 minutes at 375 degrees.
Makes 6 nice slices.

BEULAH HARRIS'S DOUBLE FREEZED ICE CREAM

2 cups evaporated milk
1 tsp unflavored Knox
   gelatin
¼ cup Karo syrup

1 tsp vanilla extract
⅓ cup sugar
2 pinches of salt

Take a half cup of the milk and sprinkle the Knox over it and let it sit for 5 minutes. Then place over low fire and stir until the gelatin has completely dissolved. Move off the heat and stir in the vanilla, salt, syrup and sugar. Then blend the remaining one and a half cups milk into the mixture. Pour into ice tray and freeze hard (approximately one hour). Remove from freezer and make small chunks of the ice cream in a chilled bowl. Beat with a electric mixer until creamy, but not melted. Pour it back in the ice tray and freeze hard, two hours at the least.

WILLADOLL'S BAKED PEEKABEEF

1 lb ground meat
2 Tbs cooking oil
3 stalks celery, chopped
2 medium onions,
   chopped
1 can cream of chicken
   soup
1 can golden mushroom
   soup

1 soup can of evaporated
   milk
1 small package of egg
   noodles
1 can chow mein noodles
½ cup toasted and salted
   pecan bits

In the oil, brown the onions, celery and meat. Stir soups and milk into the meat and mix well. Prepare noodles according to the package and mix into the beef. Pour into a big baking dish and cook, covered, at 350 degrees for about one hour. Uncover and sprinkle on the chow mein noodles and pecan bits, return to the oven for 10 more minutes.

WEE JEAN'S TURNIPED SAUSAGE CASSEROLE

½ lb loose pork sausage
1 medium head celery, chopped
7 green onions, chopped with tops
1 large sweet green pepper, chopped

2 packages dry chicken noodle soup
1 cup rice
4½ cups water, boiling
1 cup diced turnips
½ cup pecans

Lightly brown sausage. Pour off all but 3 tablespoons of the grease. Cook onions, celery, and green pepper in the sausage till tender. Salt and pepper to taste. Add the rice and soup to the boiling water and cook seven minutes. Drop in the turnips. Then mix everything together and pour into big baking dish. Cover with the pecans, put on a tight lid and cook in a 350-degree oven for one hour and fifteen minutes. Take off the lid for the last 15 or 20 minutes.

"It'll feed 'em all. But you better have all your quiltin done," Wee Jean emphasized.

EULLA PULLEN'S FIG NEWTON CREME

(Dana's Sister)

15 Fig Newtons
1 large can fruit cocktail, drained
1 Tbs lemon juice

1 tsp vanilla
1½ cups heavy whipping cream (put in freezer for 20 minutes)

Pinch each Fig Newton into fours. Mix with fruit cocktail, lemon juice, and vanilla. Whip the cream till stiff, fold into the fig mixture and serve chilled.

Serves 6.

LAYCINE DEATS'S DEEP DISH DEVIL CRAB

1 yellow onion, diced
1 medium sweet pepper,
   diced
2 eggs
1 stick oleo
1 lb crab meat, drained
   and flaked
1 cup corn bread crumbs

1 tsp French's mustard
2 tsp Worcestershire
   sauce
1 can golden mushroom
   soup
1 Tbs dry sherry wine
3 Tbs lemon juice, fresh

Fry down the pepper and onions in half of the oleo till soft. Mix all other ingredients except the eggs and corn bread crumbs into the onions and pepper. Beat up the eggs and add to this also. At once slip it all down in a good and greased deep baking dish and cover with the crumbs. Dot with what's left of the oleo and bake at 375 degrees for about 35 minutes. Make sure the crumbs, on the top, are good and brown.
Serves six ladies.

SOPHIE MAE'S PEANANA DELITE

3 smallish bananas
1 cup Sophie Mae peanut
   brittle, crushed

2 tsp vanilla
1½ cups whipping cream

Peel the ripe bananas and slice very thin. Fold into the whipped cream, the bananas, the peanut brittle, and the vanilla. Put in fancy glasses and chill.
Serves 4.

LORNA'S PRUNE CAKE

2 cups sugar
2 cups self-rising flour
3 eggs
1 tsp allspice
1 tsp cinnamon
1 tsp nutmeg

2 jars Gerber's Prune
with Tapioca baby
food
1 cup cooking oil
1 cup chopped nuts and
raisins

Mix dry ingredients. Add remaining ingredients. Bake in funnel pan at 350 degrees until done. If you don't like the spices you can leave them out.

KATHERINE BELLE'S TOMATO SOUP CAKE

1 can tomato soup
1 cup sugar
2 Tbs oleo
1 cup raisins
1 cup candied cherries,
chopped
1 cup nuts, chopped

1½ cups flour
1 egg
1 tsp cloves
1 tsp cinnamon
1 tsp nutmeg
1 tsp soda

Mix sugar, oleo, tomato soup and egg. Beat well. Sift flour, spices and soda. Add to the first mixture and mix. Add nuts and cherries and raisins and mix. Bake one hour in oven at 350 degrees. Use tube pan or leaf pan.

WILLADOLL'S HULA BREAD

2 cups flour	1 cup mashed bananas
1 tsp soda	1 Tbs grated orange rind
½ tsp salt	¼ cup milk
½ cup butter or	1 tsp vanilla
margarine	1 cup flaked coconut
1 cup sugar	½ cup chopped pecans
2 eggs	

Sift flour, soda, and salt. Cream the butter and sugar. Add eggs and beat it. Add mashed bananas, orange rind, milk, and vanilla. Stir it. Add dry ingredients. Mix it. Add coconut, pecans and bake it at 350 degrees for one hour and 10 minutes (or until it tests done) in a greased loaf pan.

Willadoll says, "If ya kinda wiggle a little while ya stirrin, it'll come out better."

BOBBIE'S LEMON/LIME JELLO CAKE SUPREME

1 box Duncan Hines	6 yard eggs
Lemon Supreme Cake	¾ cups Crisco oil
Mix	1 small box lime Jello

Dissolve Jello in 1 cup of water and add to the cake mix and blend. Add oil and blend, then one egg at a time and blend. Pour into a greased and floured tube pan and bake at 350 degrees for 1 hour. "That's Alabama time, down here in Flarda it take 30 minutes," Bobbie says.

Icing:
1 box powdered sugar
Lemon juice

Add the juice a little at the time till it's somewhere in between thick and runny. Then pour it on while the cake is still hot.

TAMMY FAYE'S TUMPED TUNA JUMP

5 potatoes, sliced
Mayonnaise
¼ cup stuffed green
   olives, chopped
1 can tuna fish, drained
   and flaked

½ cup chopped pimientos
Salt and pepper to taste
1 cup milk
1 cup crushed corn chips

Mayonnaise the potato slices and arrange (in a greased baking dish) in layers with the olives, tuna and pimientos, seasoning each layer with salt and pepper. Tump in the milk and cover with the corn chips. Bake at 400 degrees for 55 minutes. Make sure the potatoes are done before you take it out of the oven.

Perfect for a Tacky party.

ESTELL'S SHORTCUT BAKED CUSTARD

5 eggs, beaten lightly
1 can Eagle Brand
   condensed milk
3½ cups hot water
1 Tbs flour

½ tsp salt
2 tsp vanilla
Nutmeg
Margarine

Mix the Eagle brand, the flour and the hot water together. Now slowly add and stir the mixture into the eggs. Mix in the salt and the vanilla. Pour into greased custard cups, sprinkle with nutmeg and bake at 350 degrees sitting in a pan of shallow water for almost an hour. Take out of the oven and cool or chill in the icebox.

Makes 10 or 12 custard cups.

COVINA'S CURRY GREEN TOMATO CHOPS

4 good pork chops	1 Tbs curry powder
1 large onion, sliced	Salt and pepper
2 green tomatoes, sliced	Cooking sherry

In a skillet brown your salted and peppered pork chops. Place them in the bottom of a baking dish. Then layer the tomato and the onion until it's gone. Sprinkle on the curry powder, salt and pepper and a spoon or two of cooking sherry. Bake at 375 degrees for a little less than an hour.

When the girls smell the sherry in Covina's chops they all make "that" face, knowing she's trying to out-do them.

Serves 4.

CHICKEN ROSALEE

3 cups cooked chicken meat, chunked	1 cup chicken juice or bouillon
1 can chopped mushrooms	3 Tbs pimiento, chopped
⅓ cup chopped bell pepper	2 dashes Worcestershire sauce
½ stick margarine	1 tsp thyme
2 Tbs flour	Salt and pepper to taste
	½ pint sour cream

Simmer the pepper and mushrooms in the margarine and blend in the flour. Add the Worcestershire sauce, thyme, salt, pepper and the juice. Cook till thick. Add chicken and pimiento and cook for 7 more minutes. Blend in the sour cream while it's hot and serve over rice.

Serves 6.

COVINA'S PEACHES AND DREAMS

2 cups mashed peaches,
   fresh or canned
1⅓ cups sugar
1 Tbs fresh lemon juice

½ pint whipping cream,
   whipped
1 cup macaroons,
   crumbled

Mix the peaches, sugar, and the lemon juice. Fold in the whipped cream. Sprinkle the bottom of a pie tin with half of the crumbs. Pour in the peaches and dreams and cover with a blanket of remaining macaroons. Freeze 4 hours. Slices like a pie.
   Will serve 6.

POST GRAPE NUTS LORRAINE

2 bacon slices
1 cup thinly sliced
   onions
3 eggs, slightly beaten
1¾ cups milk
¾ cup (3 oz) shredded
   Swiss cheese

1 tsp salt
Dash of pepper
⅓ cup Post Grape Nuts
1 lightly baked 9-inch
   pie shell

Fry bacon. Drain and crumble. Reserve one tablespoon of drippings. Saute onions in bacon drippings until tender and browned. Combine eggs, milk, cheese, salt, pepper and cereal. Stir in onions and bacon. Pour into shell and bake at 450 degrees for 15 minutes and reduce temperature to 350 degrees and bake for 15 minutes.

FANCY-SCHMANCY TUNA NOODLE BAKE

Follow the recipe for MIDNIGHT CRUNCHY CRUMB TUNA CASSEROLE (it's on page 122), making some changes. Be sure to use solid white albacore tuna. Leave out the pimiento. Instead of cream of celery soup, use cream of asparagus. Instead of plain old egg noodles, use some color or other Italian noodles, green ones are easiest to find, but sometimes you can get a package of red, green and yellow ones. The final touch! Stir in about half a cup of Feta cheese, or even one of those French goat cheeses, and crumble some more on top before baking.

IRIS SALAD

1 can applesauce	1 Tbs sugar
1 pack lime Jello	1 small bottle ginger ale
1 tsp lemon juice	

Heat applesauce and add lime Jello and sugar, and dissolve. Cool. Add lemon juice and ginger ale. Chill.

WILLISTEEN'S SHRIMP WIGGLE

4 Tbs butter	Paprika
2 Tbs flour	Celery salt
1½ cup milk	1 egg yolk
1 cup shrimp	1 Tbs cooking sherry
1 cup peas	

Melt butter. Stir in flour and blend. Gradually add milk. Bring sauce to a boil and add shrimp. Simmer about 5 minutes. Add drained peas and season to taste with paprika and celery salt. While sauce is still simmering beat in the egg yolk and let it thicken slightly. Add sherry. Serve. The Wiggle can also be put in a casserole dish and covered with buttered bread crumbs then browned under the broiler. If mixture is too thick, dilute with some milk.

"It was so good Covina got on her horse crosswise," Willisteen said.

COVINA'S ANGELS ON HORSEBACK

1 pint oysters	12 slices bacon
½ tsp salt	⅛ tsp pepper
⅛ tsp paprika	2 Tbs parsley

Drain oysters and lay each across a half slice bacon. Sprinkle with seasonings and chopped parsley. Roll bacon around oyster and fasten with toothpick. Place on rack in shallow baking pan and bake in hot oven 450 degrees for about 10 minutes, or until bacon is crisp. Remove toothpicks and serve.

LACY'S SWEET CHOCOLATE PIE

4-oz package sweet chocolate	3-oz package cream cheese
⅓ cup milk	8-oz container of Cool Whip
2 Tbs sugar	1 baked and cooled pie crust

Heat chocolate and 2 tablespoons of milk in saucepan over low heat stirring until chocolate is melted. Beat sugar into cream cheese, add remaining milk and chocolate mixture. Heat until smooth. Cool slightly and fold in the Cool Whip. Spoon into crust and freeze until it's firm, about 4 hours. Garnish with chocolate curls.

SINKIN SPELLS, HOT FLASHES, FITS AND CRAVINS

GREENS COVER A MULTITUDE OF SINS

As told by Miss Minna Dean Winke, a maidenlady and librarian:

You know, I've never met anybody in Putnam County that hadn't heard something about Jeanette Rose Pink's awesome hot flashes. The family has made them legendary and they hand 'em down, too. You take her Aunt Jeanette Belle Pink. She had 'em terribler than her niece did. However they both found remedies and relief in many different ways, she said.

It was Belle that was notorious for undressing anyone and every-one within reach who looked the least bit too bundled-up. She'd grab 'em right at the onset of one of those flushed feelings as the heat started rising up her body. That's when she'd begin pulling at the blankets or clothes of the nearest one. She especially went for babies, Minna Dean said. She loved to free the neck area first. One time, while she was waiting in a checkout line at a local grocery store, it happened. She completely stripped a young'un still in the arms of its mother and never stopped hollerin, "My Gawd, that baby must be smothering to death, all wrapped up like that. Get them blankets off 'im 'fore I pass out right here from the heat." Another time, at a filling station, she jumped out of her car while it was still rolling, ran across the lot, and grabbed Carmilla Webber by the coat and scarf. They said, she pulled and pleaded desperately trying to convince Carmilla that she must be sweltering underneath such a pile of clothes.

But the incident which almost got 'em all sent to Chatahoo-chee, or jail, was at her oldest sister's funeral. There was poor ol Fannie, laying up in her coffin, ready to go. Belle had taken her seat in the front pew, when one of them things came over her. While she was under that devilmade fit of heat, she slipped up to the casket, and, before anyone could notice, started undoing Fan-nie's burial outfit at the neck. The family was in too much shock to do anything, if they cared at all. Finally the undertakers came and drug Belle away screaming, "Gawd lov er, Fannie must be heatin to death. Gawd lov er."

Now, I've got to hand it to Jeanette Rose Pink. She tried hard not to impose on anyone when she had a spell. She vowed never to act like Belle and tried to do different. She did, but some of her remedies were not very ladylike. She'd do the darnedest things right in mixed company. I've seen her, you can believe this if you want, gather up a big handful of skirt and start fanning herself—and I'm not talking about her face. Then, if that didn't cool things off, she'd snatch up a piece of newspaper or cardboard, the nearest thing, and begin to waffing it back and forth up under her dress. She didn't care who was around! Late one night I went over to her house to borry a cup of sugar, cause I live a couple of places down the road from her. The back door was open so I just went. . . . on. . . . in. Well, there she was sitting in a kitchen chair, as big as you please, with her legs spread and straddling the open door of the refrigerator. And, if that wasn't enough, she had the oscillating fan going . . . you know where. I couldn't believe it. She was sleeping like a baby, so I got my sugar and went home.

I'm not going to tell you the whole story but everybody knows she's got a nightgown with breakaway buttons all the way down the front. Some nights you can hear her to my house. She'll jump out of bed, scream, and run, while ripping off her gown, then land spread-eagle on top of a cold Formica table. She told somebody that it was the only thing in the house that could, really, cool 'er off. They tell me, if you have them hot flashes, you'll do anything to get relief, and Jeanette Rose just about did. But the incident that came close to putting them all in the grave, and made the inside page of the Palatka Sun, I might add, happened while Rose's two cousins were visiting here from Rolling Fork, Mississippi. Raenelle and Betty Sue were at Jeanette's house waiting for her to return from the store, when the phone rang and a mysterious voice said, "Y'all better get down to the shopping mall and pick up Jeanette Rose. . . . . she's passed out in the grocery store." And hung up. They jumped in the car and drove the quarter of a mile to the mall and ran into the store. Jeanette was just coming to when they reached her. She was still on the floor of the supermarket, with her coat pulled tightly closed. Betty Sue and Raenelle looked at each other and at the two large bulges under her coat. Raenelle flung it open to see what the lumps was. They were sure, when the lumps turned out to be bundles of collard greens and mustard greens, that she had been caught for shoplifting and fainted. "Cause that's what she went to store for," said Minna Dean.

Finally somebody came over and began to tell the girls what had gone on. It was a lady assistant manager who told her cousins the entire story of how Jeanette had come into the store acting real funny. "She kept on hangin around the frozen foods and walkin up and down in front of the freezers," the assistant manager said. "Then, after about an hour, she stopped, and, with her coat open, hovered over one of them small little freezers in the middle of the aisle, you know, the kind we put our specials in," she said. "Then up stepped Ms. so and so, that church lady, and asked Jeanette if everything was all right. She said she was just about to heat to death and was trying to keep cool. With that she slithered down the front of the of the freezer and fell into a dead faint. Her coat flew open as she fell back, leaving everything she had out in the open. I mean she didn't have nothin on except her high heels, panties and brazier," Minna Dean said the manager said.

It was then the bag boy rushed over and placed a bunch of greens over her chest and bunch of greens over her female organs, down there. Miss Winke claims it to be the gospel, by way of Paulette Huff, who said, "I seen it all." With that, Minna put her hand to her forehead, rolled her eyes, and bit down on her bottom lip.

———————

AUNT JEANETTE BELLE PINK'S OYSTER STEW
(Good for Anything)

2 cups sweet milk
2 cups coffee cream
5 Tbs butter (you got to
   have it for this one)
1 quart fresh shucked
   oysters and juice

1 tsp Worcestershire
   sauce
1 Tbs minced celery
1 tsp salt (more
   depending on the salt
   of the oysters)
Black pepper to taste

Put the butter in a saucepan and get it hot. Fry the celery until it is clear but not brown (careful butter burns easy). Add milk, Worcestershire sauce, salt, pepper and stir until hot. Pour in the oysters and simmer until they get firm but not shrivelled up. Put in bowl and cover the top with the little biddy round crackers.

It's enough for 6 with the cravin.

GOO FRANICE JAN'S

1½ lb Velveeta, cubed
   (There is no
   substitute!)
8 to 10 strips bacon, cooked
   crisp and drained

1 can tomato soup
Milk
Hot pepper sauce

In the top of double boiler, over simmering water, heat undiluted tomato soup. Add Velveeta gradually, until melted. Crumble bacon, large and small bits, into cheese and stir a lot. Add several drops pepper sauce if desired and a tablespoon or so of milk to thin, if too thick. Serve hot, out of pan, over saltines (preferred) or toast (if you want to be fancy).

It'll stick to anything.
Many servings.

MISS MACK'S JELLY JAR MILK SHAKES

Fill an almost empty jelly jar with two-thirds milk and shake. Drink right out of the jar. The kids just love 'em.

PATTINA BLAIR'S SICK SOUP

Warm milk on the stove. Add a hunk of butter and some sugar to taste. Make light bread toast, butter a bit, cut into pieces. Put toast pieces in a soup bowl and cover with the warm milk. It will cure you every time.

SOUP BEANS

(From the Big Scrub)

Take some white beans, cover with water and some baking soda. Bring to a boil. The water will turn yellow as bile. Pour off the water and repeat the process. Pour off the second water, rinse a bit. Add fresh water, some hunks of ham bone and bring to a boil, cover and let simmer till time to serve. No need to soak the beans overnight. The baking soda will take the meaness out of the beans. Soup Beans are even better if cooked the day before. Things after the second heating are always more flavorful, ain't they.

COVERED DOG PIZZA

1 package hot dogs	Oregano
½ lb sharp rat cheese	12 hamburger rolls

Split rolls. Chop up the hot dogs and cheese all together. Spread on rolls and sprinkle with oregano. Bake at 400 degrees for 10 to 15 minutes.
Makes 24.

MIDNIGHT CRUNCHY CRUMB TUNA CASSEROLE

1 small can tuna,
    drained
3 cups of cooked and
    drained noodles
1 cup celery, chopped
    fine
½ cup Hellmann's
    mayonnaise
½ cup onion, chopped
⅓ cup green pepper,
    chopped
⅓ cup canned pimiento
    Salt and black pepper
1 can cream of celery
    soup
½ cup evaporated milk
    Some kind of good
    crunchy crumbs

Mix tuna fish, noodles, celery, mayonnaise, onion, green pepper, pimiento, and salt and pepper. Stir soup and milk until heated. Pour over tuna and put in a baking dish. Bake at 400 degrees for 25 minutes, uncovered. Then add crumbs and bake till brown (5 minutes).

WAY OUT THERE GRITS

2 cups cooked grits (off
    the stove)
2½ cups sharp yellow
    cheese
1 stick margarine
2 toes garlic, chopped
    fine
2 eggs
1 little hot green chili of
    some kind (chopped
    real fine)

Beat eggs and mix everything with the grits until the cheese has melted. Bake for 50 minutes at 350 degrees.

Serves a plenty.

GERTRUDE SNIPE'S SNIPPY GRITS

1 cup grits, uncooked
1 log of garlic cheese,
    any kind
2 eggs
½ cup evaporated milk

1 stick margarine
Salt
1 cup crushed cereal,
    anything you got

Prepare grits according to box or bag. Melt the cheese (save a hunk) and the butter together then add to the grits. Beat milk with eggs and slowly stir into the grits. Salt to taste. Turn into a buttered baking dish, cover with crushed cereal. Grate the rest of the cheese on top of this and dot with lots of oleo. Bake at 350 degrees for 45–50 minutes.

    Serves six snippy ones.

AUNT JEANETTE BELLE PINK'S HOT & SASSY GRITS

2 cups cooking grits
1 cup of Jalapeno cheese,
    cubed
1½ cups Velveeta cheese,
    cut up

1 little onion, minced
1 stick of margarine
3 eggs

Cook grits according to directions. Stir in the cheeses, margarine and onion until melted. Beat the eggs and fold it into the mixture also. Pour in a greased baking dish. Bake at 325 degrees until the grits set up (about 50 minutes).

    Belle said, "You don't know whether you're havin a hot flash or not, when you eat this."

    Enough for about 6.

SUKI-WAWH-SUKI

4 cups already cooked
grits
½ lb loose sausage

2 cups cheese, melted
Buttered cracker
crumbs

Crumble the sausage and fry until brown. Pour off excess fat. Butter a baking dish and pour on half of the grits. Then add the sausage and half of the melted cheese. Cover with the rest of the grits and top with what's left of the cheese. Sprinkle cracker crumbs on the top. Bake for 20 minutes at 375 degrees.

"I don't know what this means but Jeanette Rose was justa screamin it one night while she was eatin this," Minna Dean swears.

BOILED PEANUTS

Wash your peanuts. (Hint for Yankees: don't shell.) Add one tablespoon salt to each quart of water and boil peanuts for 3 hours. They'll be soft and juicy on the inside and you won't be able to stop.

CAPTOLA'S RATTATOO-EE YOU ALL

2 large eggplants,
peeled, sliced in ¼
inch slices
Flour
Olive oil
8 medium zucchini
squash, cut into ½
inch pieces
5 large onions, thinly
sliced
6 garlic cloves, minced

6 large green bell
peppers, seeded,
diced
8 large tomatoes, peeled,
seeded, cut into strips
1 lb okra, washed and
sliced in ½ inch
slices
2 tsp thyme
2 tsp basil

Dredge eggplant slices lightly in flour and fry in olive oil over medium high heat for 5 minutes (don't crowd slices in the skillet). Drain on paper towels. Cook zucchini, onions, tomatoes, peppers, okra, garlic in the same oil until soft. Add more oil if you need it. Add the basil and thyme and blend. Layer eggplant slices and vegetables in a 6-quart baking dish. Bake, covered in a 350-degree oven for 45 minutes. Serve hot over soup bowls of crumbled corn bread.

If they ain't had a fit, they'll get one.

Serves 12.

AUNT AUDIE'S FISHY CHOWDER

1 lb frozen white fish fillets (cod, sole, haddock), thawed
1 small celery stick, sliced
2 onions, chopped
1 green pepper, chopped
2 cups potatoes, cut in chunks
5 cups Campbell's Chicken Broth
3 Tbs butter
3½ Tbs flour

Melt the butter in a pan. Add the onions and cook until soft, but not browned. Add flour and blend thoroughly. Add the chicken broth. Mix in the celery, potatoes, and peppers and season with salt and pepper to taste. Cook slowly for one hour. Add the thawed fish and cook another half hour.

"It's hard to kill a cravin, but this and biscuits'll sometimes do it," Aunt Audie said.

COOLIN OFF ICE TEA

Fill a small saucepan half full of water. Bring to boil and add a fistful of loose tea (if you can find it). Take off the fire and let sit a minute. In a tea pitcher strain the tea and squeeze all the juice out of it. Add water to the top and sweeten immediately. Serve on ice.

RACK OF SPAM

2 cans of Spam
10–12 cheese wedges

Cut the Spam in slices but don't go all the way through. You want it to open like a fan. Insert the cheese and bake at 400 till cheese is melted and the Spam is brown. Garnish with something.

WEENIES AND TORTELLINIS

½ pack wieners,
1 box tortellinis
1 cup coffee cream
2 Tbs flour

1 stick butter
Salt and pepper to taste
1 small bunch of broccoli

Chop weenies. Fix tortellinis. Cut broccoli into buds. Melt butter in a skillet. Add flour until smooth. Slowly pour in the cream. Add wennies, tortellinis, and broccoli and cook till sauce is thick and the broccoli is still bright green but tender.

TOMMIE KAY'S PEANUT BUTTER AND JELLY SOUP

½ cup chopped celery
½ cup green onions,
    finely chopped
    (including green tops)
4 Tbs margarine
2 Tbs flour
3 cups chicken broth,
    hot

¾ cup regular peanut
    butter
1 can evaporated milk
1 cup Jalapeno jelly
    (hottest you can find)
Salt and pepper

Fry onions and celery till limp but not brown in margarine. Sprinkle flour over them and stir to blend smoothly. Add chicken broth, stirring constantly. Beat in peanut butter, making sure the soup is very smooth. Season with salt and pepper. When you're going to serve the soup heat it up and quickly stir in the evaporated milk. You may not want to use it all. Make sure it doesn't boil though. Put a glob of jelly into the middle of each bowl and ladle on the soup.

BOILED COOKIES

2 cups sugar
½ cup milk
¼ lb butter or margarine
4 Tbs cocoa
2½ cups quick oatmeal

½ cup finely chopped nuts
2 tsp vanilla
½ cup crunchy peanut butter

Combine sugar, milk, butter, cocoa. Bring to rolling boil. Boil exactly one and a half minutes. Add remaining ingredients. Blend well. Press into a well greased square pan. Cool and cut into squares. Doesn't turn out too good on rainy days.

MINNA DEAN'S MOCK OYSTER DIP

1 Tbs onion, minced
1 stick butter
½ cup yellow cheese, grated
1 can cream of mushroom soup

1 small can mushroom pieces
1 package frozen chopped broccoli

Melt butter, add onion, fry until tender. Add cheese stirring until melted. Add soup and mushroom pieces. Cook 6 or 7 minutes. Cook broccoli first, drain and cool 10 minutes. Add to cheese mixture. Cook 10 minutes stirring occasionally. Serve with lots of saltines.

PAULETTE HUFF'S EASY GRASSHOPPER PIE

Crust:
6 oz chocolate wafer cookies
6 Tbs butter

Crush cookies and combine with melted butter. Press into a 9-inch pie pan.

Filling:
1½ cups whipping cream
1½ cups marshmallow
    creme

1½ oz green creme de
    menthe
½ oz creme de cacao

Combine whipped cream and softened marshmallow creme. Blend in liqueurs. Pour into pie shell and freeze at least 6 hours before serving.

LATE NIGHT DUMP CAKE

1 package yellow cake
    mix, any brand will
    do
1 1-lb can cherry pie
    filling
1 cup chopped pecans

1 1-lb can crushed
    pineapple in heavy
    syrup, undrained
1 stick of butter or
    margarine, sliced into
    thin pieces

Grease up a 9 x 13-inch pan. Spread pineapple in pan evenly. Spread cherry filling on top of pineapple evenly. Spread cake mix on top of cherry filling evenly. Put butter or margarine chips onto cake. Mix in some and sprinkle some with chopped nuts.

Bake at 350 degrees 40 to 50 minutes.

SUEULLA'S GOOFY BALLS

2 cups light brown sugar
1 cup plain flour
1 cup nuts
2 well beaten eggs

1 stick margarine
1 Tbs vanilla
confectioners sugar

Melt margarine, add other ingredients. Bake 20 minutes at 350 degrees in greased small brownie pan. Remove from oven, stir with spoon maybe twice. Do this in the next 5 or 10 minutes, or as the crust forms on top. Remove from oven while warm. Roll into small balls. Roll in confectioners sugar.

It makes you feel better just to make 'em.

DRY BEEF GRAVY

2½ oz dried beef
2 oz melted shortening

½ cup flour
1 quart sweet milk

Chop beef into fine pieces. Fry in shortening until slightly brown. Sift flour over beef and mix thoroughly. Add milk and stir constantly until thick. Serve over grits with toast or biscuits. Good for breakfast if you've got a crowd to feed.

SIMPLE SYRUP CANDY

1 large jar Alaga syrup (cane)
1 lb peanuts
3 Tbs oleo

Cook syrup and oleo over low to medium heat while peanuts are roasting in oven. Shell and skin peanuts and add to syrup. Cook over medium high heat until mixture forms a soft ball when dropped in cold water. Remove from stove and stir till you just can't wait any longer, then eat!

POTATO FIT CANDY

1 large potato   Powdered sugar
1 tsp vanilla   Peanut butter

Boil potato with jacket on, peel and mash. Add 1 teaspoon vanilla and powdered sugar until stiff like pie dough. Flour wax paper with powdered sugar. Turn candy onto paper and pat out. Spread with peanut butter, sprinkle with sugar. Roll up like a jelly roll and cut into slices.

ROSE PINK'S BALONEY ROLL-UPS

1 package baloney
1 carton orange juice
Plain yellow mustard

While standing in front of the refrigerator take one slice of baloney out of the package. Using the back of the package as your work area, tightly roll the baloney slice. Eat it and relish the salty taste or dip into the mustard and relish the salty taste! Now grab the orange juice carton and take a big swig . . . yes, straight from the carton. It's better that way. Repeat procedure until you can wait until lunch but you haven't lost your appetite. This snack is more enjoyable if, when eating, the refrigerator door is left open and you lean against the counter.

Minna Dean said, "When I found her propped-up in front of the icebox that night she still had mustard on her lips."

MAUD BOATRIGHT'S GARLICKY GRITS

4 cups milk

1 cup grits

½ cup oleo

1 6-oz roll garlic cheese

2 eggs

½ cup grated Cheddar
cheese

Bring three and a half cups of the milk to boil. Gradually stir in grits. Cook until thick stirring for 10 minutes. Remove from heat. Add oleo and garlic cheese. Stir until melted. Stir in beaten eggs and remaining milk. Pour into 2-quart casserole. Bake at 325 degrees uncovered 30 minutes or until browned. Sprinkle Cheddar cheese over top and bake about 10 minutes longer.

EATIN ON
THE GROUND

AUNT DOE RAE'S PACKAGED-UP WORLD

Aunt Doe Rae was working her mind awful hard, trying to write up an announcement of this year's homecoming-and-dinner-on-the-ground for the New Mt. Nebo Creek Baptist Church. She, especially, was trying to find the language strong enough to put a stop to the onslaught of all the cardboard cartons and Styrofoam platters of food that could be bought at any corner convenient store. She was in tears thinking about last year's dinner and how it seems that almost everyone lost the feeling and the spirit of the dinner on the ground. She knew it would take some powerful words, but at this point she was willing to say anything she could to get this occasion back on the ground. She wrote and scratched for days until she had come up with what she considered some of the dos and don'ts for a homecoming dinner. It was mostly don'ts. When she had finished, she stood up at her kitchen table and began to read it out loud, as if the entire Mt. Nebo congregation was listening.

"Do any of you, or can any of you, remember when Nuvell was just Raenelle's twin-sister, plain ol, and not some skimpy kinda French cookin. I mean, last year at our dinner, I saw a three bean salad that consisted of egxactly that! Three beans, and a sprig of somethin that looked everbit like dogfennel to me. They a-fiddlin with our fat. That's what they doin. Now, I ain't advocatin unhealthy food but what can you say against Miss Lyddie's fried pork chops, she et 'em for 96 years. And she ain't never robbed, raped er murdered nobody. She did die, but it weren't her pork chops. She simply wore out. However, take the other fence, these young folks that's been a eatin all this messa enbombed cardboard since they was knee high, they are up to their eye-teeth in dope, akahal, an devilmint. I'll tell ya, it's got to be this fast, superized eatin, cause it ain't, no matter what they say, the coloreds, the communists, nor the poor ol kudzu vine. And cholesterol was nothin compared to the the repercussion of this soulless eatin.

"Anyways, it was a shameful sight last year, at our homecomin dinner. They was cartons and boxes on every tablecloth from all the fast food stores in the county. An not a one, an I mean, not a one

135

had the decency to even cover 'em up with a nice piece of tinfoil er something. But ebem that wouldn'ta helped the taste none. Just, for instance, you take Viney's ol Chocolate Sheath Cake, she bakes it year after year after year, and then slips it down in a nest of foil on the bottom of any cutoff box. It ain't much. But, looks to high heaven. An'll melt in yo mouth, too. So you see, it... don't... TAKE ...much. I ain't askin for the sky. I'm just layin out the law this year. Not a one can bring a thing that they ain't cooked er made with their own two hands. Except for Miss Lucy, of course, she ain't got but one hand. It's got to come from your kitchen or you cain't bring it to the dinner. I don't care how many boxes and cans you use to make it, just so it come off your stove.

"Now, I'm aware that the Devil'll be workin overtime tryin to fool me, but I'll catch you, cause the Man Upstairs is gone be workin on my side. An you ladies out there, that works hard in your kitchens, I know I can depend on you to help me spot all that store-bought stuff and we'll throw it straight to the dawgs, where it belongs. Can you imagine seein Mrs. Bridie duMac's delicious Shoesoles and Grits sittin right nex ta a slice of some nasty frozen Pizza. Is that what we want our dinner affair to turn out to. No, it ain't!! An I'm puttin my foot right here to stop it. Now!! (She puts her foot out as if to trip somebody.) I know we ain't got no reason to go and get uppity about our food, cause we eat some pretty low...down...stuff ourselves. We not only eat the egg but there is them that eats "the where it come from". So, I know, we ain't fancy and we don't have all kinds a stuff that others has, but we'll take anything, and I do mean anything, an turn it till it hollers. An there is one thing you can always, just about, count on. FRESH. . . . . right off the stove, fresh. Everything from scratch, well, at least as much as you can get by with in this packaged-up world. You ain't got to mummafy food, if it's fresh made. Maybe, one warm-up, and then out it goes to the hawgs. So y'all, hear... me... good. It's them poisons in all the fast eatin that's caused this lack of pride, idle-handedness, and general no-count. It ain't the Fat. An, if I'm standin here as Aunt Doe Rae Dollar, I betcha ninety percent of them rapers, robbers and killers is skinny, skinny. An it ain't two of 'em that has ever said the blessin an eat on the ground."

AUNT DOE RAE'S RICE PUDDIN

1 cup uncooked rice	1 cup raisins
4 eggs	½ tsp ground nutmeg
2 cans sweetened condensed milk	2 Tbs vanilla

Make rice by package, fluffy and dry. Then mix it with the raisins and the milk in a pot sitting in hot water, kind of like a double boiler. Beat up the eggs (not too much) and slowly pour into the rice mixture, don't stop stirring whatever you do. Cook 6–8 minutes until it coats your spoon. Take off the fire and mix in vanilla and nutmeg. Now pour it into a dish you can take with you and shower it lightly with some more nutmeg.
   Serves 12.

CALLEEN'S CHICKEN FRIED RABBIT AND GRAVY

1 frying rabbit, cut into pieces	1 tsp salt
	½ tsp pepper
1 cup flour	1 cup Crisco

Mix together the flour, salt, and pepper in a brown paper bag. Put rabbit pieces into the flour bag, a few at a time and shake, coating them completely before frying. Heat Crisco in an iron skillet and add the rabbit pieces (do not overcrowd the skillet) and brown well on both sides. Reduce heat and cook, turning once more. Drain all but 3 tablespoons of the grease from the skillet. Add about a half cup flour and brown it, stirring and scraping up the brown bits from the bottom of the skillet. When the mixture is browned, add one and a half cups water slowly, stirring. Cook over low heat until gravy is thick.

FRIED MEAT, SAWMILL GRAVY, AND CATHEAD BISCUITS

Wash a pound or so of salt pork and slice to a quarter inch. Put in a black iron skillet and cover with water and bring to a boil. Drain the meat and rinse again to get rid of what's left of the salt. Then cook the salt pork in the skillet, slowly, until golden brown. Drain on paper. Pour off all but two or three tablespoons of the grease from the skillet and turn the heat up to medium. Add about three tablespoons of flour and brown. Mix a quarter cup of water and three fourths cup of milk. Add slowly to the skillet, stirring constantly. Salt and pepper it to taste and bring to a boil at medium heat. Good served over hot Cathead Biscuits.

CATHEAD BISCUITS

2 cups White Lily self-rising flour
½ cup lard
¾ cup buttermilk

Cut in shortening till it looks like meal. Add enough milk to make the dough come away from the sides of the bowl. Knead on a floured surface 10 or more times. Pinch off 6 to 8 good-size pieces and roll into biscuits no more that three quarters inch thick. Place on an ungreased baking tin and put in a preheated 450-degree oven for 15 minutes or until golden brown and big as cat heads.

Make your biscuit, meat and gravy sandwiches before you leave home. They'll be good and juicy by the time they're served.

Will serve four or more, depending on their appetites.

FRIED CORN

9 fresh corn ears
½ cup bacon drippings
1 cup half and half cream
   (sweet milk will do)

Salt and pepper to your
   taste

With a sharp knife run down the cob and slice off all the corn. Then scrape the cob until all the corn juice is removed. Into a hot black iron skillet add the drippings. When it sizzles add the corn stirring a lot so it doesn't stick or burn, but it should get a little crispy. Cook till thick (6 or 7 minutes), don't stop stirring. Pour in the cream, salt, pepper. Put a lid on it and cook slow for 10 to 15 minutes more. Cool it and take it right on to the dinner.
Serves 4.

MISS QUEEN'S CRACKLIN CORN BREAD

2 cups self-rising
   cornmeal
1½ cups buttermilk
1 egg

1 Tbs melted Crisco
1 cup cracklins or crispy
   fried bacon crumbs

Add the buttermilk and egg to the cornmeal, stirring until blended. Fold in cracklins and half of the Crisco. Pour batter into a sizzling hot, well greased skillet (the one with the rest of the melted Crisco). Bake at 450 degrees for 25 minutes. Wrap it up good to keep it hot!
Will serve 6.

RACHEL MOODY'S FRIED CHICKEN WITH
MILK CREAM GRAVY

1 2½-lb fryer, cut up	¼ tsp pepper
1 cup flour	1½ cups butter-flavored
1 tsp salt	shortening

Put flour, salt, and pepper in a grocery bag. Drop in the chicken, roll up the bag and shake until all pieces are coated. Make sure to hold a hand on the bottom of the bag. Heat shortening in an iron skillet and place the pieces of chicken into the hot fat (careful not to splash the grease), turning often to brown. After browning the chicken, cover skillet and cook about 20 minutes. Remove the lid and cook another 10 minutes. Drain on paper towels. Serve with Milk Cream Gravy.

To make milk cream gravy: drain off the fat from the skillet, except for five tablespoons, saving all the crispies. Stir in two or three tablespoons of flour till smooth. Slowly add two cups of milk. Stir and thicken. Salt and pepper to taste.

Sometimes I pour my gravy right over the chicken in the skillet. There's always a batch of biscuits or cake of corn bread to sop it up.

MARTHIE'S MT. NEBO DRESSED CHICKEN

2 lbs cooked and boned chicken meat	1 can cream of celery soup
½ stick oleo	1½ cups chicken broth (saved from the boiled chicken)
1 box corn bread stuffing mix	
½ cup evaporated milk	

Put chicken meat in a deep cast iron Dutch oven or other pot. In a saucepan melt oleo and combine with soup and milk till hot. Pour over the chicken. Mix the corn bread stuffing with the chicken broth and spoon over the chicken mixture in the Dutch oven while it is on the fire. Don't stir it up. Bake for 25 minutes in 425-degree oven or until the dressing is brown.

Make certain you take a big spoon to dish it out.

TURNIP GREENS, POT LIKKER, AND CORNMEAL DODGERS

2 bunches turnip greens
2 quarts cold water

½ lb chopped country
    ham
1 Tbs oil

Fry ham in a pot large enough to hold all the greens. Wash turnip greens in two or three waters (to git rid of the grit). Cut off tough stems, bruised and wilted leaves. Add the greens to the frying ham and cook covered until completely wilted and seared on the bottom. Add 2 quarts of water and slow boil till greens are tender (30 or 40 minutes). Season the greens with salt and pepper to taste and keep hot on stove until dodgers are ready to cook.

Cornmeal dodgers: mix 1 cup white self-rising cornmeal and a half teaspoon salt. Cut in two tablespoons melted shortening. Slowly mix four or five tablespoons cold water until it makes a dough that can hold its own shape. Make biscuit size dodgers and gently lay on top of the boiling pot likker and greens. Bring up to a boil, turn down the heat, put a lid on and simmer about 20 minutes.

Makes 6 dodgers.

FRANCEEN'S GOOD OL MEAT

1 can Spam
  Cracker crumbs
  (saltines, of course)

2 beaten eggs
  Crisco and butter (or
  just either one)

Slice Spam into 6 or 8 pieces. Roll in finely crushed crumbs and then into egg and back in crumbs again, pressing firmly. Let sit awhile. Melt shortening and/or butter in skillet and fry Spam slices until golden, turning once or twice. Good with ketchup or chili sauce. Serve hot. Cold leftovers make good sandwiches with white bread and Miracle Whip.

Franceen Jance said she's seen 'em sneak these into the Kentucky Derby when she lived there.

MISS FAITH RIVER'S PLEASIN PAPPY CAKE

The reason this is called a 'Pleasin Pappy Cake' is because it makes such a good, sturdy batter. So, whatever cake pleases Pappy you can bake him in a jiffy, by just shifting around the ingredients. Strawberries, chocolate, apples. You name it!

Basic Cake:
  2 eggs
  10 Tbs butter
  1⅔ cups sugar
  2¾ cups plain flour

1½ tsp baking powder
1 tsp vanilla
1¼ cups milk

Soften the butter, then cream with sugar. Add eggs. Add baking powder, vanilla, and then mix in the flour and the milk, a little of each at a time till all used up. Beat till it looks smooth. Pour into two layer pans, or tube pan, or one 9 x 12-inch pan, that has been greased and floured. Bake at 350 degrees till lightly browned and knife comes out clean when stuck in middle of cake.

Icing:

1 box 10X powdered
   sugar
1 stick butter

1 tsp vanilla or almond
   flavoring
A little bit of milk

Mix first three ingredients and enough milk to make it look like icing. Spread on cooled cake.

For strawberry cake, add half or a third a carton frozen strawberries. Put the rest of them in the icing, but leave off the milk, use some of the juice for liquid. Add some extra sugar if you think it needs it. For chocolate cake, mix in 3 or 4 melted squares of semi-sweet chocolate or 3 to 4 tablespoons of cocoa. Same amount of melted squares or cocoa for the icing. Pappy wants an apple cake? Then stir two cups thinly sliced apples and one cup finely chopped walnuts into the batter. Makes a delicious moist cake. Ice it with half cup butter and a package of cream cheese, an eight ounce one, all whomped up with some chopped walnuts too.

BEE BEE FLICK'S COVERED DISH CHICKEN

Meat from 1 cooked
   and boned chicken,
   chopped
2 cups cooked rice
4 celery stalks, chopped
1 small yellow onion,
   chopped
1 cup mayonnaise
3 hard-boiled eggs,
   chopped

2 cans Campbell's
   Golden Mushroom
   Soup
½ cup pecans, chopped
1 Tbs French's mustard
1 cup cracker crumbs
1 tsp salt
2 Tbs melted margarine

In a casserole dish mix everything except bread crumbs and melted margarine. Stir together the bread crumbs and the melted butter and sprinkle over the top of the casserole and bake at 350 degrees for 40 minutes or until it bubbles.

HILLIE'S LEMON CHESS PIE

3 eggs, well beaten
1 stick of butter
1½ cups of sugar
1 Tbs cornmeal

1 Tbs white vinegar
1 tsp lemon extract
Pie crust, uncooked

Cream butter and sugar. Then stir in cornmeal and eggs. Add flavoring and vinegar. Pour into pie crust and bake at 350 degrees until firm.

Hillie Manes says this is so good it'll make you drop yo drawers.

JW'S DOUBLE CHEESE CASSEROLE

1 lb sharp grated
    Cheddar cheese
1 lb cottage cheese
6 eggs, beaten
¼ tsp nutmeg
¼ tsp cayenne pepper
1 cup Bisquick

1 garlic clove, pressed
1 cube chicken bouillon
½ cup dry, not sweet,
    sherry wine
½ cup milk
½ cup melted butter

Mix together the cheeses and eggs. Add the cayenne, nutmeg, garlic, and Bisquick to the cheese mixture and blend thoroughly. Heat, but don't boil the sherry wine and dissolve the chicken bouillon cube. Mix the sherry mixture with the milk and add to the cheese mixture. Pour half the melted butter into a casserole and add the other half to the cheese mixture and blend thoroughly. Pour into the casserole and bake for 40 minutes in a 350-degree oven.

Serves 6.

VADA MILDRED'S PAN FRIED MULLET

Clean and scale the mullet but leave him whole. Any pan-size fish will do. Salt, pepper and a little bit of cornmeal on each side.

On an open fire heat up the black iron skillet with a good amount of grease in it. When it's hot drop in the mullet and fry until crispy and brown. Drown him in lemon juice and serve.

Aunt Doe Rae said, "Vada did this right at the dinner and they come all the way from Jawga for 'em."

MISS LYDDIE'S FRIED PORK CHOPS

12 pork chops, rubbed with a small amount of brown sugar
Salt and pepper to taste
Flour (enough to cover them good)

Heat Crisco shortening in a cast iron skillet and fry the chops to a golden brown. Pile up on a platter, cover and they are ready to go to the dinner.

MARY LOU GURR'S THUMP SALAD

4 cups mashed potatoes, leftover, seasoned and a little dry
¼ cup diced celery
¼ cup diced green pepper
¼ cup diced onion or scallions

2 hard-boiled yard eggs, chopped
5 or 6 Tbs of mayonnaise
3 tsp mustard

Mix potatoes, mayonnaise and mustard thoroughly. Fold in the celery, peppers, and onions. Then the eggs (eggs last so as not to mash the yolks). Taste for seasoning. Add more mayonnaise if it's too dry. Best served at room temperature or you can chill it.

TWO DINNER BEEF STEW POT PIE

2 lbs of stew beef
2 Tbs shortening
1 large onion
3 carrots

3 medium potatoes
Flour
Salt and pepper

Dredge salted and peppered beef in flour. Fry in shortening until brown. Add enough water to cover. Turn down heat, put a lid on and cook meat until tender. Add onions, carrots, and potatoes and again cover with water. Cook until vegetables are like you like them. Salt and pepper to taste. Serve.

POT PIE

Take what's left of the beef stew and add a package of frozen peas to it. Sometimes you need a little more juice too. Heat it up on the stove to a bubble. Cover with homemade biscuits and put in hot oven for 10 or 20 minutes (when the biscuits are brown).

Biscuit Dough:
2 cups self-rising flour
¼ cup lard
Sweet milk

Cut lard into the flour until it looks like a coarse meal. Add a little milk at the time, enough to make a thick dough. Roll out on a floured surface and cut biscuits with the end of a Calumet can.

ROOSTER AND DUMPLINS

Kill and dress the rooster. Cut in pieces and put in a pot that has a cover. Cover with water. Add one teaspoon salt and a half teaspoon of black pepper, more if you like it. Cover and stew slowly until the meat begins to fall off the bone. Take out the meat and remove the bones. Add enough flour dissolved in water to thicken the broth. Then return the meat to the pot.

Dumplins:

2 cups flour
4 tsp baking powder
  Milk

2 Tbs rooster fat
  (skimmed from the
  pot)
½ tsp salt

Mix flour, salt and baking powder. Cut in the fat with a fork or something. Add milk a little at the time until a thick drop batter is formed. Spoon onto the boiling chicken until dough is all gone. Cover and boil for 12 minutes. It takes that steam to cook little fluffy dumplins. Drop by tablespoon if you like big ones and a teaspoon if you like little ones. Take it right off the stove and put it on the back seat and head for the dinner. It's also good for company comin.

AUNT MILDRED'S MUSTARDS

2 bunches of mustard
  greens
  Lean ham hunks

3 chicken bouillon cubes
  Salt and pepper to taste

Rip all the leaves from the stems and wash at least 3 times maybe more. If you miss a stem here and there, don't worry, some people like a little stem. Fry the ham hunks in a big pot and put in the mustards. When they are all wilted, add water to cover, bouillon and cook till tender.

"They not so fatty," Aunt Mildred said.

AUNT DOE RAE'S BUTTERMILK POUND CAKE

1 cup shortening
2 cups sugar
4 eggs
2½ cups plain flour

½ cup self-rising flour
1 cup milk
1 Tbs butternut flavoring

Cream shortening, sugar and eggs for one minute. Blend flours. Add half of flour to creamed mixture. Beat one minute. Add milk and remaining flour. Add flavoring and beat well. Bake at 325 degrees for one hour. Increase heat to 350 degrees and bake 10 minutes more.

Icing:

1 box powdered sugar
½ cup shortening
1 Tbs butternut flavoring

Blend sugar and shortening. Add flavoring. Add enough milk to make it easy to spread out icing on cooled cake.

BRIDIE DUMAC'S SHOESOLES AND GRITS

3 or 4 thin cubed steaks the
size of a shoesole
1 small onion, chopped

1 can stewed tomatoes
4 cups cooked grits

Flour and fry steaks. Cook down onions and tomato. Make grits by directions on bag. Grease a glass loaf dish and put a layer of grits and a steak and a layer of tomatoes. Repeat till gone. Top with grits. Let sit till firm and slice like meat loaf.

PREACHER'S WIFE'S BUTTERSCOTCH DESSERT

First layer:
1 cup flour
1 stick butter
½ cup chopped pecans

Mix together and press into 9 x 13-inch pan or two pie shells. Bake at 325 degrees for 15 minutes. Then cool.

Second layer:
1 8-oz package cream cheese
1 cup powdered sugar
1 cup Cool Whip

Beat well the cream cheese and sugar, then add Cool Whip and spread onto first layer.

Third layer:
1 package instant vanilla pudding
1 package instant butterscotch pudding
3 cups milk
1 Tbs vanilla

Mix well and let stand until thick and spread over second layer. Top with more Cool Whip and refrigerate.

This was not accepted at Mt. Nebo when she first come here.

VINEY'S CHOCOLATE SHEATH CAKE

2 cups sugar	½ cup buttermilk
2 cups self-rising flour	2 eggs
1 stick oleo	½ tsp cinnamon
½ cup oil	2 pinches salt
4 Tbs cocoa	1 Tbs vanilla
1 cup milk	

Sift together sugar and flour into large bowl. Place oleo, oil, and cocoa, milk into saucepan. Bring to rapid boil. Pour over flour and sugar, beating well. Mix together buttermilk, eggs, cinnamon, salt, and vanilla and pour into other mixture. Mix well and put into greased pan. Bake at 400 degrees for 20 minutes.

Icing:

½ cup nuts	6 Tbs milk
1 tsp vanilla	4 Tbs cocoa
1 stick oleo	1 box powdered sugar

Put all ingredients except sugar in saucepan and bring to slow boil. Add sugar and spread on cake while it is still warm.

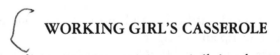

WORKING GIRL'S CASSEROLE

6 medium potatoes	1 lb hamburger
1 cup grated cheese	½ cup chopped onion

Cook and mash potatoes till creamy. Put in a casserole and using spoon hollow out hole in center about the size of a saucer. Brown loose hamburger and onions. Fill hole in potatoes with hamburger and onions. Cover with grated cheese. Place in oven at 450 degrees until cheese melts and is bubbly and you're ready to eat. It travels good too.

GRAMMA WHITT'S FAMOUS FLAP JACK

2 cups self-rising flour
½ tsp soda
¼ tsp sugar

2 Tbs Crisco shortening
1½ cups buttermilk

Sift dry ingredients into a mixing bowl. Mix well. Add buttermilk and shortening. Stir until the liquid is mixed enough to pour the batter into a greased pan. Bake at 400 degrees until brown.

She just takes a big platter of them to the dinner and serves 'em with milk gravy.

LYNN WOOD'S COMPANY CHICKEN

A cut-up chicken
Flour
Salt and pepper
Apple, sliced
Green peppers, sliced

Onion, chopped
White raisins
Butter
White wine
Slivered almonds

Dredge chicken in flour, season with salt and pepper, and fry until nice and brown. Put in a casserole in layers with the apples, onions, and green peppers. Pour over all this some white wine, enough that you can just see it below the top layer. Dot with hunks of butter. Top with almonds. Cook covered in oven at 375 degrees for an hour. Uncover and cook another 15 minutes to brown almonds.

Lynn said, "It's better if you fix it the day before and let it sit in the icebox overnight then heat it up for your company."

VINEY'S VINEGAR PIE

1 stick margarine,
   melted and cooled
2 Tbs flour
1½ cups sugar

1 Tbs vanilla
2 Tbs vinegar
3 whole eggs
1 9-inch baked pie shell

Combine margarine, vanilla, sugar, flour, vinegar, and eggs. Pour into pie shell. Bake at 300 degrees for 45 minutes.

Eat Your Meat

HOPPIN' JOHN

½ cup diced salt pork
1 onion, chopped
2 cups cooked black-eyed peas
2 cups cooked rice
1 can stewed tomatoes

Sauté the pork until done. Remove it from the pan and cook the onion, until tender, in the drippings. Mix your peas, rice, tomatoes, and salt pork in with the onion. Simmer for about 30 minutes.

BAKED POSSUM AND SWEET TATERS

1 possum, cleaned
Salt
Pepper
Sage
6 sweet potatoes, peeled and sliced

Rub the possum with salt, pepper, and sage. Place it in the oven and bake it, covered with a small amount of water, for 2 to 2½ hours at 325°. Add your sweet potatoes about 45 minutes before the cooking time is up. As Ernie Mickler says in *White Trash Cooking,* "You can only eat possum in the winter."

STICK TO YOUR RIBS BEEF STEW

According to the fellas at a popular Georgia hunting camp, take 2 pounds of bottom round and cut it in 1-inch cubes. Then brown 2 tablespoons of fat. Use the drippings to brown 2 chopped onions and 2 stalks of diced celery. When they are brown, stir in 3 tablespoons of flour and enough water to make a paste. Add 1 tablespoon of salt, ¼ teaspoon of butter, 1 bay leaf, and a pinch of ground cloves. Cook stew for 1 to 2 hours over a low flame. Serve over white rice.

SQUIRRELS À LA KING

Soak 2 dressed squirrels in salt water overnight to freshen them up. An hour or two before dinner, wash them rascals in 2 changes of cool water. Throw them in a kettle with enough water to cover. Add the 2 halves of an onion, some celery, salt, and pepper; then bring to a boil. Skim the surface foam from the bubbling stew and let it simmer until done. Drain and dry the squirrels. Then split them down the back and brown the 4 halves in a buttered skillet until golden brown. This is best served with cabbage.

HUNTING CAMP STEW

4 squirrels, or 2 chickens
½ pound raw bacon
1 large can stewed tomatoes
3 pounds potatoes
4 large bell peppers
1 small can English peas
1 clove garlic, chopped
1 can corn
2 pounds onions, chopped
1 pound crisp bacon
Dash of hot sauce (optional)

Cut the meat into small pieces and simmer it with raw bacon in enough water to cover. Cook until the meat separates from the bone. Take out the bones and add the rest of your ingredients. Let the stew simmer for 4 to 5 hours, or even overnight in a crockpot. You can add hot sauce to the stew if you like it with a little zest. "It's better than snuff and not half as dusty."

FRIED COOTER

When the cooter sticks his head out, cut it off with a hatchet. Then open him up down the sides of his shell. Skin his legs out and wash the meat. Salt, pepper, and flour the cooter meat and fry it in a deep grease in a deep-fat fryer, just like chicken. When the meat's done, it will float to the top. Cooters are also known as freshwater turtles, but the folks up around northwest Florida call them Suwannee river chickens. In Florida, cooter season runs between August 1st and April 14th.

*Bless the meat and
Darn the skin,
open your mouth
and cram it in!*

BUBBA'S BOURBON CHICKEN

4 boneless chicken breasts
¾ cup bourbon
2 tablespoons brown sugar
2 tablespoons soy sauce
2 tablespoons lime juice
⅓ teaspoon nutmeg
   Pinch of red pepper
⅛ teaspoon ginger
   Pinch of cumin
   Cooking oil

Dice up your chicken into cubes and place it in a 11 by 7-inch baking dish. Marinate the cubes for about 30 minutes in the mixture of bourbon, brown sugar, soy sauce, lime juice, nutmeg, red pepper, ginger, and cumin. In a skillet, heat up your oil and sauté the chicken until it is golden brown. Eat this over white rice with some of the marinade juice to soak through.

COOTER KEBABS

2 pounds of raw cooter
½ cup salad oil
⅓ cup vinegar
1 medium onion
1 teaspoon salt
¼ teaspoon pepper
7 green bell peppers

Open up your cooter's shell with a hatchet, like in Fried Cooter, clean and separate the meat, and cut the meat in 1-inch cubes. Combine the salad oil and vinegar. Grate your onion into the oil and vinegar. Then add the salt and pepper. Add the meat and cover. Let the meat stand for 4 hours, then drain. Cut the bell peppers into squares. On 8 skewers, string the meat alternately with peppers. Place the skewers on a broiler rack with the top 3 inches above the electrical unit or the tip of the flame. Broil for about 15 minutes, being sure to turn the kebabs several times.

LU LU'S LEFTOVER TURKEY SHORTCAKE

1 tablespoon butter
1 tablespoon cornstarch
½ cup diced leftover turkey
½ cup leftover broth or gravy
¼ teaspoon salt
  Pepper to taste
½ cup milk

In a pot on low heat, add all of the ingredients. For desired thickness, add more or less milk. When the mixture is hot, pour it between biscuits.

HAMBONE'S HAM DUMPLIN'S

1 cup flour
1 teaspoon baking powder
¼ teaspoon chopped rosemary
1 cup cooked ham, diced
¼ cup milk
  Pinch of salt

Sift together ¾ cup flour, baking powder, and rosemary. Add the ham, then milk, and shape the mixture into small balls. Roll them in the remaining flour and drop them in hot stew with the salt. Cover the pot tightly and cook 12 to 15 minutes without removing the cover.

FLEW THE COOP CHICKEN SOUP

4 pounds white chicken meat
8 cups water
2 carrots
2 small onions, chopped
2 celery stalks, diced
1 bay leaf
1½ teaspoons salt
Pepper to taste

Add the ingredients in a big ol' pot and let them simmer on the stove for about 2½ to 3 hours. This runs a darn close second to Grandma's Tater Soup and is still the best remedy for whatever's ailing you.

JEPTHA'S VIDALIA HASH

2 large Vidalia onions
3 tablespoons fat or salad oil
1 pound ground round
1 can stewed tomatoes
½ cup uncooked rice
1 teaspoon chile powder
1 teaspoon salt
Pepper to taste

Slice the onions and brown them in the fat. Add the meat and brown that. Then add the tomatoes, rice, chile powder, salt, and pepper. Cover and cook slowly for 30 minutes, or until the rice is tender. Continue to stir the hash occasionally.

LUCY BELLE'S FUNKY CHICKEN CASSEROLE

1 package seasoned stuYng mix
1 cup water
1 stick butter, melted
2½ cups chicken, cooked
½ cup onion, chopped
½ cup celery, chopped
½ cup mayonnaise
¾ teaspoon salt
2 eggs, slightly beaten
1½ cups milk
1 can cream of chicken soup
3 cups Cheddar cheese, grated

Mix the stuffing mix, water, and butter together. Put half of the mix into a casserole dish. Now, mix the chicken, onion, celery, and mayonnaise together. Sprinkle with salt and pour it in the dish, on top of the bread mixture. Now combine the rest of the stuffing mixture with the eggs and milk and pour on top. Refrigerate overnight. Take out the casserole 1 hour before baking and spread chicken soup over the top. Bake this uncovered at 350° for 40 minutes. Now, remove the casserole from the oven and coat the top heavily with your grated cheese. Put it back in the oven for another 10 minutes, or until the cheese melts.

STRAIGHT FROM THE BUTCHER BEEF JERKY

2½ pounds of salt
¾ pound barbecue sauce
½ cup soy sauce
4 tablespoons black pepper
¾ cup vinegar
2 lemons, or ¼ cup lemon juice
¼ cup Worcestershire sauce
3 tablespoons garlic powder
3 ounces of liquid smoke
4 tablespoons crushed red pepper
   (for hot jerky, add 4 tablespoons cayenne)
1 large bottom round

In 1 gallon of hot water, add all the ingredients except the meat and let the mixture dissolve. Then add 4 gallons of cold water and stir well. Now, take 2 5-gallon pails and put half the mixture in each. Take 1 large bottom round and cut meat against the grain, in small, thin slivers. Soak the cut meat in the pails. Cover the pails and refrigerate for three days, stirring the mixture every day. After 3 days place your meat strips across the smoker racks. Dry the meat and let it cool.

Beef is more commonly used but turkey jerky is my favorite.

MISS DIXIE'S CASSEROLE

  6 hard-boiled eggs
  ½ pound sliced boiled ham
1½ cups whole kernel corn
  1 can chicken corn chowder
  ½ cup bread crumbs
     Butter

Slice the eggs and place half of them along with half of your ham into the bottom of a casserole dish. Add the corn and soup, then the remaining eggs and ham, and top with the bread crumbs. Dot the top with butter and bake the casserole at 400° for 20 to 30 minutes.

ONNIE JANE'S COTTON-PICKIN' CHICKEN PERLOW

1 large chicken
1 medium onion, chopped
½ bell pepper, diced
1 clove garlic, diced
1 medium can tomato paste
1 cup water
2 cups rice
  Salt
  Pepper

Boil your chicken until it's tender. Throw the bones away, but reserve the 4 cups broth. Set chicken meat side. In a medium skillet sauté onion, bell pepper, and garlic. Then add tomato paste and water. Let this mixture simmer until it cooks down. Now, in a big ol' pot, pour in 2 cups of rice and the reserved chicken broth. Add the chicken meat and the tomato mixture in with the rice. Let this boil, covered, for about 10 minutes. Then stir. Put the lid back on for about 20 minutes, or until the rice is done. Onnie says, "Don't let the rice get gummy or gritty." Use salt and pepper if desired. You can also substitute sausage or lean pork for the chicken.

WILLIE'S HILLBILLY PIE

2 pounds ground beef
6 potatoes, or 1 box of instant
    mashed potatoes
1 can corn
1 can green beans
¼ teaspoon salt
¼ teaspoon pepper
1 8-ounce package grated Cheddar cheese

Brown your beef in a skillet, then drain and set aside. Make mashed potatoes as you normally would or follow instructions on the box. Open the cans of veggies and drain them. In a baking dish, start making layers, beef on the bottom, then your corn, beans, mashed potatoes, salt, and pepper. Take the cheese and pour it on top of the potatoes and bake the pie at 350° for 20 minutes, or until the cheese melts.

NANNY'S SUNDAY MEAT LOAF

½ cup bread crumbs
1 cup tomatoes, diced
2 pounds ground beef
½ cup onion, chopped
¼ cup bell pepper, diced
2½ teaspoons salt
2 teaspoons Worcestershire sauce
Pinch of oregano

Soak the bread crumbs in the tomatoes until soft. Mix with the meat, onion, pepper, and seasoning. Mold the mixture into a loaf and put it into an oblong baking pan. Bake the loaf at 350° for approximately 90 minutes. Not only is this meat loaf delicious on Sunday, it's even better the next day as sandwich meat.

CAPTAIN HEYWOOD'S CONCH CHOWDER

```
 6  ounces diced salt pork
 1  large onion, chopped
 1  bell pepper, chopped
 1  7-ounce jar pimentos, drained
 3  large stewed tomatoes
 3  garlic cloves, minced
 2  celery stalks, chopped
 2  potatoes, peeled and diced
 2  tablespoons parsley
 2  pounds conch meat
 1  cup dry white wine
10  cups clam juice
 1  teaspoon pepper
¼  teaspoon hot sauce
    Salt to taste
```

Cook the salt pork over medium heat until the fat's cooked out. Leave the remaining cracklings in the pot. Add the onion, bell pepper, pimentos, maters, garlic, celery, potatoes, and parsley. Cook, stirring often, until the vegetables are tender and the onion is clear. Grind your conch meat, and then add the wine, clam juice, pepper, hot sauce, and salt. Don't forget to throw in the conch meat. Boil and reduce heat. Cover and let the chowder simmer until the potatoes have cooked down and thickened the chowder.

KENTUCKY BURGOO

1 fat stewing chicken
2 pounds each of beef, pork, and
    veal shanks
3 tablespoons salt
6 each of potatoes, onions and carrots,
    peeled and sliced
2 cups each of diced celery, okra, corn,
        lima beans, and chopped green cabbage
1 green pepper, diced
    Dash each of cayenne, hot pepper sauce,
        steak sauce and some Worcestershire sauce

Put the meat in a 20-quart stockpot and cover it with cold water. Bring the water to a boil. Cover the pot and reduce the heat. Then let it simmer for 3 to 4 hours, or until the meat falls off the bone. Remove the meat and throw out the bones. Let the meat cool. Then dice it up and put it back in the stew. Throw in the rest of the ingredients and let the burgoo simmer until it gets thick. "Now, remember to stir this concoction a lot in the beginning and more near the end," says Clyde "Junior" Montgomery, of Hazard, Kentucky.

HOG JOWL WITH TURNIP GREENS

1 pound mustard greens
½ pound fresh hog jowl
1 pound tender turnip tops
Water

Wash and drain your greens. Put them in the pot with the meat and add just enough water to cover. Simmer covered until the meat is tender. Wash and drain your turnip tops and put them in a separate pot with about 1 cup water and let them simmer until tender. Now, add your turnip tops along with their juice to the mustard greens and meat. Simmer for 10 minutes, then drain and keep the juice. The juice is called "Pot Likker."

AUNT PEARL'S FROG LEGS

16 large frog legs
 3 cups boiling water
   Juice of ½ lemon
   Salt
   Pepper
 2 eggs, beaten
 2 cups dry bread crumbs
   Vegetable oil or fried meat's grease

Put them legs in boiling water with lemon juice, salt, and pepper. Boil the legs for 5 minutes. Then drain water and pat the legs dry. Dip the legs in eggs and crumbs. Heat the fryer to 370°, with enough oil to cover the legs, and drop them in. Let them fry for 2 to 3 minutes, or until they are golden brown and tender. Pearl says, "Those legs'll be hoppin' higher in the fryer than they were in the pond."

FIVE-ACRE ROAD BEER RIBS

Take 1 slab of ribs and cut off the excess fat. Put them in a pan with enough beer to cover ribs. Soak ribs in beer overnight in the fridge. Before you cook, while ribs are still in the beer, add a dash of each of the following: seasoned salt, "Everglades" seasoning, cumin spice, garlic powder, and black pepper.

Throw the ribs on the grill and baste them with a brush, using the above beer and spice mixture, basting every time you turn ribs on the grill. Approximately 5 minutes before ribs are done, add your favorite barbecue sauce to the ribs.

VENISON HASH

2 tablespoons cooking oil
1 pound ground venison meat
1 onion, diced
½ bell pepper, diced
1 can stewed tomatoes
¾ cup long-grain rice
½ cup water
1 teaspoon chile powder
1 teaspoon salt
¼ teaspoon black pepper

Heat up your oil in a skillet and brown the meat, onion, and bell pepper. Pour in the rest of the ingredients and mix well. Now, pour the mixture into a greased, covered baking dish. Bake at 350° for 45 minutes.

WILD BILL'S DEER BURGERS

1   pound ground venison
½   pound ground sirloin
2   teaspoons garlic powder
2   teaspoons seasoned salt
2   tablespoons teriyaki sauce
    Salt and pepper to taste

Mix all the ingredients together and then form the meat into patties. Place the patties on a grill and cook them until done, depending on how you like your burgers. This is one of my dad's greatest inventions.

VENISON STRAPBACK

Butterfly your strapback by cutting the meat ½ to 1 inch thick across the center, so when you open the fillets, it's almost in two, like a butterfly's wings. Presoak the fillets in milk and 2 tablespoons of teriyaki sauce and refrigerate overnight. To prepare, pat dry and add garlic powder and ground cumin to taste. Cook over a hot grill about 1 minute on each side. Do not overcook the meat. This is the best part of the deer.

SUNNY GIRL'S CHICKEN GUMBO

1½ pounds chicken breast
1½ pounds ham
 2 tablespoons salad oil
 4 cans stewed tomatoes
 1 large onion, chopped
 ½ cup bell pepper, chopped
 2 packages frozen okra
 2 quarts water
   Hot sauce to taste
   Salt and pepper to taste
   Rice (optional)

In a large pot, brown the chicken and ham in salad oil. Then add the rest of the ingredients and more water, if necessary. Bring to a boil and reduce to simmer for 1½ to 2 hours. When the gumbo is ready to serve, you may add 2 cups of cooked rice or pour it over rice.

REVEREND HASKELL'S DEVIL CRABS

> 1 large onion, chopped
> ¾ cup bell pepper
> 3 cloves garlic, minced
> 2 tablespoons olive oil
> ¾ can tomato sauce
> 3 to 4 dashes of hot sauce
> 2 cans crabmeat
> 1½ cups Italian bread crumbs
> ¼ cup Parmesan cheese
> Egg whites and cracker crumbs

Brown the onion, bell pepper, and garlic in oil. Then add the tomato sauce and hot sauce. Mix the crabmeat, bread crumbs, and cheese. Form the mixture into rolls and refrigerate them for 4 to 5 hours, or overnight. Before frying the rolls, beat 2 egg whites to form stiff peaks. Dip the crab rolls in the egg whites and cracker crumbs. Deep-fat fry the rolls until they are golden brown. Lordy!

MICKLER'S SMOKED MULLET

Cut the fish from head to tail, leaving the scales on. Clean the inside cavities well. Salt the fish lightly and apply Old Bay seasoning generously. Put the mullet in a smoker until the fish meat splits from the bones. It's ready to pick and eat.

SMOKED MULLET DIP

1½ pounds smoked mullet
1¼ cups mayonnaise
  2 tablespoons chopped parsley
  2 tablespoons chopped sweet pickle
  1 tablespoon mustard
  2 teaspoons dried minced onion
  2 teaspoons finely chopped celery
  1 clove of garlic, minced
    Dash of Worcestershire sauce

Remove skin and bones from the fish. Flake the fish well. Combine all of the ingredients, mix well, and chill at least 1 hour. Spread dip on a Ritz cracker and wash it down with an RC Cola.

SAM'S REDFISH CHOWDER

Take 6 pounds of redfish (filleted) and roll them in cornmeal and fry 'em. Then take a broiler and 2 cans of Veg All, an extra can whole corn, and 1 can of tomato chunks. Let the vegetable mix simmer for 10 minutes by itself. Pick the meat off the bones and add the vegetables to the skillet. Let the chowder simmer over a low heat for 20 minutes. Adding hot peppers is optional. Eat up!

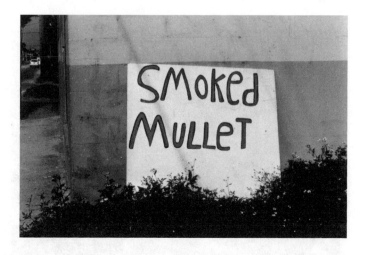

UNCLE PERCY'S PEEL AND EAT BEER SHRIMP

Take 2 pounds of fresh shrimp and wash them well. Into a big pot, pour 4 cans of the beer of your choice and 1 cup of water. Bring that to a boil. Then add the shrimp. Dash in the spices of your choice. Percy uses garlic powder and a bit of cayenne pepper. When the shrimp have turned a bright pink, they are done. The alcohol cooks out of the shrimp, but you're left with a great flavor. Drain the shrimp; then peel and eat. Percy says, "If these ain't the best shrimp you ever tasted, I'll go to hell in a handbasket!"

SMOTHERED IN LOVE DOVES

        6 doves
        6 tablespoons butter
     1⅓ tablespoons flour
        1 cup chicken broth
           Salt and pepper to taste
       ¼ cup cooking sherry

Brown the doves in a buttered skillet. Transfer the doves into a baking dish, breast-side down. Add your flour to the skillet, then stir well. Slowly, add the broth, salt, pepper, and sherry. Blend the sauce well and pour it over the doves. Cover the doves and bake them at 350° for 1 hour.

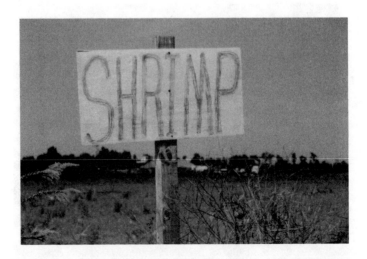

COUNTRIFIED FRIED CHICKEN

Cut 1 fryer into pieces. Salt and pepper each piece. Combine ¾ cup of flour, 1 teaspoon of salt, and ¼ teaspoon of pepper in a plastic bag. Shake each one until they are coated well with the flour mixture. You can fry chicken in a deep-fat fryer, covered, for 5 minutes, then uncovered, until coating is golden brown. Turn chicken occasionally.

You can also fry chicken in a skillet on your stove. My grandma always fried her chicken in fried meat's grease and a pinch of garlic salt.

COUSIN CLEM'S FRIED GATOR TAIL

After you skin your gator, clean and cube your meat. Soak it overnight in milk and 2 tablespoons of teriyaki sauce. Salt and pepper to taste. You may add other seasonings depending on how spicy you like your tail. Roll it in cornmeal and fry it until it is golden brown. Clem told me, "This is a mighty popular dish with Florida State Seminole fans."

HANK'S MOCK HAM LOAF

2   pounds ground beef
1   pound hot dogs, ground
2   teaspoons salt
¼   teaspoon pepper
2   eggs
2   cups crushed crackers
1½   cups brown sugar
1   teaspoon dry mustard
2   cups water

Mix the first 6 ingredients together. Make your syrup by mixing the brown sugar, mustard, and water together. Save ½ cup of the syrup and add the rest to the ingredients. Place the meat mixture in a baking dish and pour the remaining syrup over the top. Bake at 350° for 90 minutes. Hank says, "If they cain't taste the difference, don't tell 'em."

AUNT NENE'S CHURCH SOCIAL CASSEROLE

>   2 tablespoons oleo
>   3 tablespoons flour
> 1½ cups milk
>   ½ teaspoon salt
>   2 cups Cheddar cheese, grated
>   1 cup spaghetti, broken up
>   3 cups raw cabbage, shredded
>   1 pound ground beef, browned

Melt the oleo and stir in the flour. Slowly add milk and salt to make a white sauce. Grate your cheese and mix in 1 cup. Cook the spaghetti and drain. Layer cabbage, beef, and spaghetti in a baking dish. Make holes in the cabbage mixture and pour white sauce over the top. Bake covered for 30 minutes. Add the remaining cheese and put the casserole back in the oven uncovered for 15 minutes.

MAMA SUTIE'S HIALEAH HASH

1 pound ground beef
1 medium onion, chopped
1 clove garlic, diced
2 tablespoons cooking oil
5 or 6 medium potatoes, peeled and cubed
½ to 1 cup water
Salt and pepper to taste

Brown your beef and drain the fat. Meanwhile, sauté the onion and garlic in the cooking oil. Then, in a big skillet, add them in with the beef. Next, throw in the potatoes and pour in the water. Cover and let the mixture cook over medium heat until the potatoes get done. Salt and pepper to your liking. Sutie told me, "Slap some mayonnaise on some bread and eat it along with it. It's a meal in itself!"

BUCK SHOT'S GRILLED CHICKEN LIVERS AND GIZZARDS

1 pound chicken livers
1 pound chicken gizzards
  Seasoned salt
  Garlic powder
  Cumin, ground
  Everglades seasoning
  Teriyaki sauce

Wash your livers and gizzards. Get two big pieces of aluminum foil, and put your livers on one and your gizzards on the other. Dash on your salt, powder, seasonings, and teriyaki sauce. The amount you add depends on how spicy you like it. Wrap sides tightly to keep the juices from spilling out. "Put on a grill, and cook for 10 minutes on one side, turn for another 10 minutes on the other side, one more turn for another 10 minutes and they'll be done. Be sure you don't poke a hole in that foil, or you'll have an awful mess," says Buck, from Thonotasassa, Florida.

Taters, Maters, 'n' Greens

TATER SANDWICH

Slice your taters fairly thin and fry them in a greased skillet until they're golden brown. Slap them between 2 slices of bread (toasted is my favorite), mayonnaise optional, sprinkle some bacon bits on top, and eating don't get any better.

TATER SOUP

5 or 6 taters cut in squares
Butter to taste
Salt to taste

Bring half a pot of water to a boil. Throw in the taters, and when they get soft, start mashing them up. Add your butter and salt to what suits you. You can add milk to make it richer, or cornmeal to thicken it up. Guaranteed to get rid of the mully grugs.

SCREAMING MEME'S TATER SALAD

5 medium taters
2 tablespoons mayonnaise
2 teaspoons relish
  Datil pepper relish to taste
3 hard-boiled eggs
1 celery stalk
1 bell pepper
1 small onion

Peel and cut your taters into squares, boil them until they're soft, and drain. Put them back in the pot and stir in the mayonnaise, relish, and datil pepper relish to taste. Cut up the eggs, celery, bell pepper, and onion. Mix all the ingredients together. With too much datil relish, you'll know why Meme's screaming!

DRUNK SWEET POTATOES

3 cans sweet potatoes
1 cup sugar
⅓ cup bourbon
½ cup butter
½ teaspoon vanilla extract
2 cups mini marshmallows

Throw the potatoes in a large saucepan over medium heat, stirring until heated through. Preheat the oven to 350°. Then, mash the sweet potatoes and add the sugar, bourbon, butter, and vanilla. Beat until well blended. Transfer the mixture to a 2-quart baking dish and sprinkle with marshmallows. Cook for 30 minutes.

MARGARET ELISE'S MATER GRAVY

2 or 3 eggs
    1 can tomatoes, stewed
    1 pound bacon or Italian sausages

Cook the eggs until they're almost solid. Then mix in the tomatoes. Season with bacon, or the sausages of your choice. This is best if eaten over white or yellow rice, or even better, grits.

OKRA SUCCOTASH

    3 cups okra
    ⅓ pound bacon
    1 cup chopped onion
    1 cup chopped bell pepper
    1 tablespoon garlic, minced
    2 cups tomatoes, chopped
    1 cup corn
      Salt to taste

Boil and drain your okra to get the slime off. In a large skillet, brown the bacon. Add the onion, pepper, and garlic. Now mix in the okra and stir. Next, throw in the tomatoes, corn, and salt. Succotash should simmer on low for about an hour.

TICKLED PICKLED OKRA

2 pounds fresh okra
5 pods hot peppers
5 cloves garlic, diced
2 tablespoons salt
1 quart white vinegar
1 tablespoon celery seed
½ cup water
5 canning jars

Wash the okra and pack it into hot, sterile jars. Place a pod of pepper and a clove of garlic in each jar. Combine the other ingredients and bring them to a boil. Pour the mixture over the okra and seal the jars tightly. Okra pickles should stand at least 2 weeks before using.

UNCLE GAYNARD'S TRUCKER BEANS

1 pound ground beef
½ cup water
1 package Lipton Onion Soup mix
1 cup brown sugar
1 medium can tomato sauce
1 teaspoon mustard
2 cans baked beans
1 can kidney beans
1 can butter beans
Salt and pepper to taste

Brown your meat and add ½ cup of water. Next, pour in the soup mix and blend well. Add the rest of the ingredients and bake the beans for 90 minutes at 350°.

FLORIDA EGGPLANT CASSEROLE

1 large or 2 small eggplants
2 tablespoons onion, chopped
4 tablespoons butter, melted
1 teaspoon salt
¼ teaspoon white pepper
1 pinch oregano
1 pinch thyme
2 eggs, beaten
¼ cup milk
1 cup crisp bread crumbs

Peel and dice the eggplant and boil it until it's clear and tender. Cook the onion in 2 tablespoons of butter until the onion is soft; then set it aside. Mash the eggplant, and you'll have at least 2 cups of pulp. Add the seasonings, eggs, milk, and onion. Put the mixture in a 1-quart baking dish and top it with bread crumbs and the rest of the butter. Bake at 350° until golden.

FRIED GREEN TOMATOES

4 to 6 green tomatoes
      2 tablespoons brown sugar
      1 cup flour
      1 cup bread crumbs
      ¼ cup milk
      1 egg, beaten
      3 tablespoons butter
      1 tablespoon oil

Slice the green tomatoes about a ½ inch thick. Mix the sugar, flour, and bread crumbs together and place the mixture in a shallow bowl. Dip both sides of the tomato slices in the dry mixture. Next, in a separate bowl, combine the milk and egg. Dip the tomato slices in this mixture and once more in the dry mixture. Heat up your butter and oil in an iron skillet and fry your tomatoes to a golden brown on both sides.

PUTNAM COUNTY POTATO PANCAKES

4 large potatoes, pared
¼ cup onion, grated
2 eggs, beaten
2 tablespoons flour
¾ teaspoon salt
  Pinch of nutmeg
  Pepper to taste
2 teaspoons oil

Grate the potatoes and make sure you have 3 cups. In a large bowl, throw together the potatoes, onion, eggs, flour, salt, nutmeg, and pepper. In an iron skillet, heat up your oil very hot, but not smoking. For each potato pancake, drop 2 tablespoons of the mixture in the hot oil. Flatten the cakes with a spatula to make them about 4 inches long. Fry them 2 or 3 minutes on each side, until golden brown.

SWEET POTATO CASSEROLE

  2 cups sweet potatoes, mashed
¼ cup brown sugar
  1 teaspoon salt
½ teaspoon cinnamon
  1 cup mandarin oranges, drained
1½ cups mini marshmallows

Combine the sweet potatoes, brown sugar, salt, and cinnamon. Whip them with a mixer until fluffy. Then fold in the oranges and marshmallows. Bake the casserole in a greased casserole dish for 30 to 40 minutes at 350°.

SWAMP CABBAGE

Cut 1 medium swamp cabbage in crossways strips. Put cabbage and ½ cup water in a pot on medium heat. Let the cabbage get tender. Meanwhile, simmer some salt pork in a separate pot. When the cabbage is tender, drain and add the salt pork. Simmer together for about 15 minutes. This is Skeeter Allen's wife's swamp cabbage recipe. He said, "There ain't nothin' that can touch Ray-etta's cabbage!"

OH MY GOSH SQUASH PIE

    1 cup cooked squash
    ⅔ cup sugar
    3 tablespoons flour
    ¾ cup milk
    1 tablespoon butter
    2 egg yolks
    1 teaspoon lemon flavoring
    1 unbaked pie shell

Throw in the first 6 ingredients and cook them until they are slightly thick. Add the lemon flavoring, pour it all into a pie crust, and bake it at 350° for 30 minutes.

OKAHUMPKA OKRA SOUP

1 large whole beef bone with plenty of meat on it
3 quarts water
2 medium onions, chopped
3 pounds fresh okra, or 5 10-ounce packages
     frozen okra
2 tablespoons salt
½ teaspoon pepper
2 bay leaves
8 tomatoes, diced
½ pound sliced bacon, chopped fine

Boil the beef bone in enough water to cover. Then skim the fat from the surface of the water. Remove the bone and cut the meat into small pieces. Throw the meat in a pot with 3 quarts of water, along with the onions, okra, salt, pepper, bay leaves, tomatoes, and bacon. Add 2 more cups of water, if needed. Simmer this for 2 hours, stirring occasionally.

PEANUT CORN CHOWDER

  2 tablespoons butter
  ½ cup celery, chopped
  ¼ cup onion, chopped
  ½ cup chunky peanut butter
  1 can chicken broth
  2 cans of corn, drained
  1 cup light cream
     Salt to taste

Melt the butter in a saucepan. Then sauté the celery and onion until tender, about 5 minutes. Remove from heat and add the peanut butter. Stir until it's melted. Gradually stir in the broth and the corn. Bring to a boil, still stirring, reduce heat, and simmer uncovered for 10 minutes. Remove from heat. Stir in the light cream and reheat gently, without boiling.

BEULAH MAE'S CORN PUDDING

  2 tablespoons sugar
1½ tablespoons cornstarch
  1 cup milk
  3 eggs, beaten
  1 can cream corn
  2 tablespoons butter
  ½ teaspoon salt
    Pinch of nutmeg

Mix together the sugar and the cornstarch. Slowly add the milk, stirring until smooth. Add the eggs, corn, butter, and salt. Mix well. Pour the mixture into a greased 1-quart baking dish. Sprinkle the top with nutmeg. Now, place your baking dish in a pan of hot water and bake at 300° for 90 minutes, or until the custard is set. Beulah says, "This is bound to be the best corn puddin' this side of Cairo, Georgia."

POTATO SAUSAGE CASSEROLE

2 pounds pork sausage
1 can cream of mushroom soup
½ cup onion, chopped
¾ cup milk
½ teaspoon salt
¼ teaspoon pepper
3 cups uncooked potatoes, peeled and cubed
8 ounces Cheddar cheese, grated
  Chopped fresh parsley, for garnish

Brown the sausage, drain it, and set it aside. Combine the soup, onion, milk, salt, and pepper. In a greased 2-quart casserole dish, layer ½ of the potatoes, ½ of the soup mixture, and ½ of the sausage. Cover the dish and bake at 350° for 1 hour, or until the potatoes are tender. Sprinkle the casserole with cheese and return it to the oven uncovered for 2 to 3 minutes and let the cheese melt. Garnish with parsley.

CLETUS AND THELMA'S STUFFED PEPPERS

6 bell peppers
½ pound ground beef
½ cup canned tomatoes, diced
1½ tablespoons onion, minced
1 cup cooked rice
  Salt and pepper to taste
1 cup water
2 cups mozzarella cheese

Wash and cut the top from your peppers. Then remove the seeds. Brown your beef and drain the fat. Mix the beef, tomatoes, onion, rice, salt, and pepper. Then stuff the peppers with the mixture. Set the peppers in a baking dish, pour hot water around them, and bake them at 350° for 40 minutes. Grate your cheese and sprinkle it evenly over the top of the peppers. Put them back in the oven for about 5 minutes, or until the cheese melts. Cletus swears that a dash of Tabasco makes it better, but Thelma says, "Don't you do it. It'll ruin the whole darn thing!"

HUBERT'S MAMA'S GARLIC EGGS

4 eggs, separated
¼ cup evaporated milk
½ tablespoon garlic powder
   Butter or cooking spray

Mix the first 3 ingredients together and pour them in a preheated buttered skillet. Scramble eggs 3 or 4 minutes, or until they aren't runny. You can eat the eggs by themselves or slap them between two pieces of toasted bread for a garlic egg sandwich. "Foller this recipe an' you'll keep evil at bay for at least two days!" says Hubert's mama, Mrs. Zora Lee.

GOOD OL' BLACK-EYED PEAS

4 cups fresh black-eyed peas, shelled
3 cups water
1 ham hock
1 onion, chopped
½ teaspoon salt
¼ teaspoon pepper

Throw all of these ingredients in a big pot and bring the water to a boil. Reduce the heat and cover. Let it simmer for 30 minutes, or until the peas are tender. If you need to, add more water. That will keep the peas from sticking to the pot.

MAMA'S FRIED OKRA

Wash about 1 pound of fresh okra. Cut the ends off of each piece, then slice. In a plastic bag, coat the wet pieces of okra in cream meal and salt. Shake! Now, in a hot skillet, fry the okra in bacon grease until golden brown.

BIBLE BELT BOILED PEANUTS

Take about 2 pounds of fresh raw peanuts, wash them, and put them in a large pot on the stove with enough water to cover them. Bring the water to a boil. Add salt to your liking. The bigger the nuts, the longer it will take them to boil. When the peanuts are tender, drain them and eat up! Everyone in the South adds their own unique touch to their boiled peanuts. For some, it's hot sauce and peppers, and for others, it might be bacon or turnip tops. Below the Mason-Dixon line, peanuts are often called goobers!

TOMATO FRITTERS

2 cups tomatoes, chopped and cooked
2 eggs, beaten
1½ cups cracker crumbs
¼ cup onion, minced
½ teaspoon salt
⅛ teaspoon pepper
1 teaspoon sugar
1 tablespoon butter

Add all the ingredients together and stir well. Drop them by spoonfuls into a hot, buttered skillet. Brown the fritters on both sides and eat them while hot.

SISTER RUBY'S POLE BEANS

3 strips bacon
½ cup onion, finely chopped
1 pound fresh pole beans
1 cup water
2 chicken bouillon cubes
½ teaspoon basil
¼ teaspoon salt
¼ teaspoon pepper

Fry your bacon until crisp; then drain. Cook the onion in the bacon drippings for about 2 minutes. Add the beans, water, bouillon cubes, basil, salt, and pepper. Cover and let simmer for 15 minutes. Crumble your bacon over the top.

REBEL CABBAGE CASSEROLE

1 head cabbage
1 pound ground beef
1 onion, minced
½ cup rice
1 teaspoon salt
¼ teaspoon pepper
1 medium can tomato soup
½ cup water

Chop your cabbage in large pieces and put it in the bottom of a greased 2-quart baking dish. Brown the meat and onion together; pour off the fat. Still in the skillet, mix the rice, salt, and pepper with the meat and onion. Then pour all of that mixture over the cabbage. Cover with soup and water. Cover and bake at 350° for 1 hour.

EFFIE'S HASH BROWN CASSEROLE

2 pounds frozen hash browns, thawed
8 ounces sour cream
2 cups Cheddar cheese, grated
1 can cream of chicken soup
1 teaspoon salt
Pepper to taste
½ cup margarine
2 cups crushed Ritz crackers

Combine the hash browns, sour cream, cheese, soup, salt, and pepper.
Mix well. Spread the mixture in a 9 by 13-inch baking dish. For
the topping, mix the margarine with the cracker crumbs and spread
it over the top of the casserole. Bake the casserole at 375° for 30 to
40 minutes.

Grits, Corn Bread, and
and
Everythang Else

GRITS CASSEROLE

1 cup uncooked grits
2 eggs
1 10-ounce package American cheese
1 stick margarine
1 tablespoon seasoned salt

Cook the grits as directed on the box. Beat the eggs slightly. Grate the cheese and mix with the remaining ingredients. Pour it all into a greased baking dish and cook it at 350° for 30 minutes.

Also good: Cut up bacon, sausage, or ham and throw it in.

POKE ROLLS AND GRITS

Poke your feet under the table,
Roll your eyes, and
Grit your teeth.

DOWN-HOME BISCUITS

2 cups flour
1 teaspoon salt
3 teaspoons baking powder
6 tablespoons shortening
⅔ cup milk

Mix the flour, salt, and baking powder. Cut or rub in shortening, add milk to make dough soft, knead it lightly, and roll it ¼ inch thick. Cut the biscuits with an upside-down pint jar or a tuna can with top and bottom removed. Bake them at 450° for 15 minutes, or until golden.

For buttermilk biscuits, follow the same recipe, except use buttermilk in place of milk. Use only 2 teaspoons of baking powder and add ¼ teaspoon of baking soda.

CRACKLIN' CORN BREAD

¾ cup self-rising flour
¾ cup self-rising cornmeal
¼ teaspoon of salt
1 egg
6 strips of fried crisp bacon, or ¼ cup cracklings
 Buttermilk

Mix the flour, cornmeal, salt, and egg together. Drop in the bacon or cracklings. Pour in enough buttermilk to make the mixture thick, but not soupy. Pour the mixed batter into a hot cast-iron skillet. Put in the oven at 400° until the corn bread is a golden brown.

GRAMMA RODDENBERRY'S CORN-BREAD DRESSING

    4 cups stale bread, cubed
    4 cups corn bread, crumbled
    1 onion, minced
    2 cups celery, chopped
    4 tablespoons butter
    8 cups chicken broth
    4 eggs, beaten
    2 tablespoons sage
    2 teaspoons salt
    1 teaspoon black pepper

Combine all of your bread cubes and crumbs. Brown the onion and celery in butter until tender and add this to the bread mixture. Now, pour in the broth, eggs, and seasonings. You may need more broth, depending on the dryness of your bread. Bake the dressing about 45 minutes at 400°.

AUNT BESSIE'S BAKED MAC AND CHEESE

½ pound macaroni, uncooked
½ pound grated Cheddar cheese
2 tablespoons butter
2 eggs, beaten
2 cups milk
½ teaspoon salt

Cook your macaroni as directed on the box, or until the noodles are soft, but not gummy. Drain the noodles and layer the macaroni and cheese in a baking dish. Next, add the butter. Beat the eggs and mix them with milk and salt. Pour this over the macaroni. Bessie sprinkles some cheese on the top and lets the dish set for about 30 minutes. Then put mac and cheese in the oven for 1 hour at 350°.

ELMO'S HUSH-UP PUPPIES

1 cup cornmeal
½ teaspoon salt
3 teaspoons baking powder
¾ cup buttermilk
1 tablespoon sugar
1 tablespoon flour
¼ teaspoon baking soda
1 egg, beaten
½ onion, chopped
¼ bell pepper, chopped

Combine all the ingredients and drop the dough by spoonfuls in hot fat in a deep-fat fryer. Cook until the puppies are golden brown. Elmo says, "These are mighty good with fried catfish and tomato gravy and rice."

SKEETER'S BUTTERED GRITS

2¼ cups grits
1 teaspoon oil
4 cups boiling water
½ cup butter

Add the grits and oil to boiling water. Stir some, then cover with a tight lid. Cook on low heat for 15 to 20 minutes. Take the pot off the fire and let it stand for 5 to 10 minutes. Now, add your butter while your grits are still hot.

COUSIN CECIL'S CHEESE GRITS

    1 cup grits
    1 teaspoon salt
  3¾ cups boiling water
  1¼ cups grated Cheddar cheese

Pour the grits slowly into salted boiling water, stirring constantly. Let it boil as you keep stirring for 2 minutes. Cover the pot, reduce the heat, and cook the grits for 2 to 3 more minutes. Take the grits off the heat. Then add the cheese and let it melt. Serve it hot. Cecil says, "This is so good, even Yankees will like it!"

HONEY LAMB BISCUITS

1 egg
½ teaspoon salt
1 teaspoon baking soda
1 cup sour cream
1 cup sugar
2 cups flour
1 cup strained honey
1 cup whipped butter

Mix everything up good and pour it in a greased and floured muffin pan. Bake at 350° for 10 to 12 minutes, or until golden.

FRIED SQUASH BREAD

2 summer squash
1 cup cornmeal
1 egg
¼ cup buttermilk

Wash, clean, and dice 2 summer squash. Cook them until they are soft, but don't dry them out. Leave about ¾ cup water in the pot. In a bowl, combine the cornmeal, egg, and buttermilk. Now, add squash and water to the other ingredients. Fry in hot oil until golden brown.

WHEEZER'S CHEESE PIE

1 cup shredded Cheddar cheese
1 cup mozzarella cheese
1 cup Monterey jack cheese
1 onion, chopped
2 tablespoons all-purpose flour
4 eggs
1 cup milk
½ teaspoon salt
½ teaspoon dry mustard
½ teaspoon Worcestershire sauce
2 tomatoes, sliced

Mix the cheeses, onion, and flour. Spread the mixture in a greased pie plate. Beat the eggs lightly and then beat in the milk, salt, mustard, and Worcestershire sauce. Pour this over the cheese mix and bake the pie uncovered at 350° for 35 to 40 minutes. When it's done, let it stand and top it with tomato slices.

MADEL'S MONKEY BREAD

1½ cups sugar
 4 tablespoons cinnamon
 ½ cup butter
 3 cans biscuits
 1 cup brown sugar
 ½ teaspoon honey

Stir together all the ingredients and cook the biscuits as directed on the package, but take them out before they get done and sop them in the mixture above. Put them back in the oven and let them get done. Madel says, "I've been making monkey bread for my young 'uns since they were knee-high to grasshoppers."

CHACHI WACHI'S COTTAGE EGGS

4 eggs
3 heaping tablespoons cottage cheese
Ham (optional)
Salt and pepper to taste

Mix the eggs in a bowl. Scramble the eggs and, when they're almost done, mix in the cottage cheese and ham. Then finish cooking until the eggs are done. The mixture will look soupy, and you can drain it if you like, but we don't. Make some honey-buttered toast and sop it up.

BUMPKIN PUMPKIN BREAD

3½ cups sugar
 3 cups flour
 1 teaspoon cinnamon
 1 teaspoon cloves
 1 teaspoon allspice
 1 teaspoon baking powder
 1 teaspoon baking soda
 4 eggs
 1 cup oil
 1 can canned pumpkin
 ½ cup nuts
 ½ cup raisins

Mix all the ingredients. Butter and flour 3 clean coffee tins. Fill each tin halfway and bake the bread at 350° for 1 hour.

STRAWBERRY-FIG PRESERVES

> 3 cups cooked figs
> 1 6-ounce package strawberry-flavored Jell-O
> 2 cups sugar

If dark figs are used, the preserves will be dark (peel the figs for lighter preserves). Thoroughly mix the figs, Jell-O, and sugar in a saucepan. Bring the mixture to a boil over medium heat and let it cook for 15 minutes, stirring occasionally. Pour it quick into hot, sterile jars and seal the jars with hot paraffin wax.

DONALD'S DATIL PEPPER JELLY

    2 bell peppers
    2 datil peppers
  1½ cups cider vinegar
    6 cups sugar
    2 3-ounce packages of Certo liquid fruit pectin

Throw out the seeds from the peppers. Finely grind the peppers in a blender or food processor. Add the vinegar and sugar, and in a saucepan, bring the mixture to a boil. Stir constantly. Skim the top and add the Certo. Boil another minute. Then pour the jelly into your canning jars. Datil peppers are peppers found on the northeast coast of Florida and Georgia. They are extremely hot! Donald told me, "You'll have to take a crap in the creek so you won't set the woods on fire!"

CORN FRITTERS

1 tablespoon vegetable oil
1 egg, beaten
1 cup milk
1 cup canned corn, drained
1 small onion, chopped
2 cups all-purpose flour
½ teaspoon salt
¼ cup sugar
1 tablespoon baking powder
  Powdered sugar for dusting

In an iron skillet, heat 2 inches of oil to 350°. In a medium bowl, combine the egg, milk, corn, and onion. Blend the flour, salt, sugar, and baking powder into a separate bowl. Stir the egg mixture into the flour mixture and blend. Drop the batter by spoonfuls in the hot oil. Fry for 3 to 5 minutes, or until golden brown. You can also cook these fritters in a deep-fat fryer in about the same amount of time. When the fritters are done, drain them on a paper towel, let cool, and then sprinkle with powdered sugar.

MERTON'S FAMOUS CHEESE SPOON BREAD

    1 cup cornmeal
    1 teaspoon salt
    2 cups water
    2 tablespoons butter
 1½ cups shredded sharp cheddar
    1 cup milk
    3 eggs, separated
       Pinch of cayenne powder
    1 teaspoon baking powder

In a bowl, mix the cornmeal and salt. In a medium saucepan, bring 2 cups water and the butter to a boil. Now, add that to the cornmeal mixture, stirring with a wire whisk. Add the cheddar cheese and stir until it is melted. Add the milk and beat until it's smooth. Let the mixture cool. Preheat the oven to 375°. Lightly grease a 2-quart casserole dish. In another bowl, beat the egg whites until stiff peaks form. In another small bowl, beat the yolks until light. Now, fold the egg whites, yolks, cayenne, and baking powder into the cornmeal mixture until well mixed in. Pour this into the casserole dish and bake the bread for 1 hour, or until it is golden brown.

CAST-IRON SKILLET CORN BREAD

1 cup flour
4 tablespoons baking powder
1 teaspoon salt
1 cup cornmeal
2 eggs, beaten
¼ cup bacon drippings
1 cup milk
3 tablespoons sugar

Preheat the oven to 425°. Grease the bottom and side of a cast-iron skillet. Then put it in the oven while you're preparing the batter. Sift the flour, baking powder, and salt into a bowl. Add the cornmeal and blend the ingredients with a spoon. Add the eggs, drippings, milk, and sugar. Lightly stir all the ingredients. Remove the skillet from the oven. Then pour in the batter. Bake for another 20 minutes, or until a broom straw poked in the center comes out clean.

VEDA'S SPICY TOMATO BREAD

2½ cups flour
1 tablespoon baking powder
¾ teaspoon salt
1 teaspoon garlic salt
¼ teaspoon cayenne pepper
1 teaspoon oregano
¾ tablespoon sugar
1 cup Cheddar cheese, grated
1 cup Parmesan cheese, grated
1 can stewed tomatoes, chopped
⅓ cup milk
2 eggs
¼ cup vegetable oil

Sift the flour and the baking powder, and mix in the salt, garlic salt, cayenne pepper, oregano, sugar, and cheeses. Drain the juice from the stewed tomatoes, saving ⅓ cup. Mix the ⅓ cup tomato juice with your ⅓ cup of milk, then pour into the flour mixture. Now, combine the eggs and oil and stir well; add this to the flour mixture and stir. Add the chopped tomatoes. This batter will be thick. Bake the batter in a loaf pan for 1 hour at 350°.

MASHED POTATO BISCUITS

1 teaspoon salt
1¾ cups flour
1 cup butter, chilled
2 tablespoons sour cream
1 cup cold mashed potatoes
4 egg yolks

Mix the salt and flour and slice in the butter. Add the sour cream, potatoes, and 3 egg yolks. Then blend. Knead together the dough and roll it into a ball. Chill it until it is firm. Repeat the kneading and chilling process. After chilling the dough, roll it out to ¼ inch thick. Brush the dough with the remaining egg yolk; cut the dough with a 2-inch biscuit cutter. Bake the biscuits at 400° for 15 minutes or until golden.

PEANUT BUTTER BACON BREAD

1 cup sugar
2 tablespoons shortening
1 cup milk
1 egg, beaten
1 cup peanut butter
½ teaspoon salt
2 cups flour
3 teaspoons baking powder
1 cup peanuts, unsalted
1 cup fried bacon

Mix together the sugar, shortening, milk, and egg. Add the peanut butter. Mix in the salt, flour, and baking powder. Now, pour in the peanuts and the crumbled bacon. Let the dough stand for a few minutes in a greased and floured loaf pan. Bake the bread at 350° for 1 hour, or until a broom straw comes out clean.

CORNMEAL DUMPLINGS

2 cups cornmeal
1 tablespoon baking soda
1 teaspoon salt
½ pound raw sweet potatoes
½ cup flour
4 quarts water

Mix the cornmeal, baking soda, and salt. Peel and grate your sweet potatoes. Add the potatoes, along with the flour, to the cornmeal mixture. Boil the water and add enough of it to the dry mix so it sticks together like biscuit dough. Pinch the dough into small pieces and mold it like biscuits. Drop them in the remaining boiling water. Cook the dumplings until they float.

MAISY RAE'S PLANT CITY STRAWBERRY BUTTER

    1 cup fresh strawberries
    2 cups butter
    ⅓ cup powdered sugar
    Dash of vanilla

Blend all the ingredients together in a blender, making sure you blend it real good. Store it in a mason jar and keep it in the fridge. If you want to make a lot for later, it can also be frozen. Maisy has eaten this every morning on her toast for the last eighty years.

UNCLE EARL'S BEER PANCAKES

2 cups biscuit mix
½ teaspoon cinnamon
½ cup beer
2 tablespoons sugar
4 eggs, beaten
2 tablespoons oil

Mix all the above ingredients together. The batter will be lumpy. Use about ¼ cup batter for each pancake. Cook each pancake until golden brown. Earl says, "For thinner pancakes, pour in more beer."

BEER MUFFINS

¾ cup beer
1 tablespoon sugar
2 cups biscuit mix

Heat the oven to 400°. Grease the bottoms of your muffin tins. Mix all the ingredients up real good for about 1 minute. Fill the tins ⅔ full. Bake the muffins until golden—12 to 15 minutes ought to do it.

Warning: Be sure that you exclude these two recipes from any church function you may be attending.

BOBO'S CHEESE LOG

1 cup American cheese
½ cup pimentos, drained
8 ounces cream cheese
½ cup pecans, chopped
   paprika

Soften the cheese to room temperature. Then mix everything together. This will make 3 balls. Then shape them into logs. Sprinkle the logs with paprika, and you can also roll them in an extra layer of nuts. Chill overnight.

BUTTERMILK PANCAKES

2 cups flour
1 tablespoon sugar
2 cups buttermilk
½ teaspoon salt
1 teaspoon baking soda
1 egg
1 teaspoon baking powder

Combine all the ingredients and mix real good. Chill the batter overnight. Cook the batter on a greased skillet until the pancakes are golden and full of bubbles.

NED'S GONE FISHIN' MIX

4 cups mixed bite-sized cereal squares
2 cups rolled oats, uncooked
2 cups pretzel sticks
1 cup Cheddar goldfish crackers
1 cup mixed nuts, dry roasted
2 tablespoons bacon drippings
¾ teaspoon salt
½ teaspoon pepper
3 tablespoons vegetable oil
3 tablespoons Worcestershire sauce
¼ teaspoon hot sauce

Preheat your oven to 350°. In a baking dish, toss in the cereal along with the oats, pretzel sticks, crackers, and nuts. In another bowl, mix the rest of the ingredients. Then drizzle them over the mix. Toss quickly. Bake the mix for 15 minutes, or until it is crisp and golden. Stir the mix occasionally while it is baking. Ned swears, "You'll be so busy eatin' this, you'll forget to bait your hook!"

DADDY'S DATIL PEPPER RELISH

3 large bell peppers
6 large onions
1 clove garlic, minced
2 cups datil peppers, seeded
1 gallon tomato ketchup
3 cups vinegar
2 cups white sugar
1 cup brown sugar
1 tablespoon salt

Grind the bell peppers, onions, garlic, and datil peppers together in a blender or grinder. Then, in a large pot, combine mixture with the ketchup, vinegar, sugars, and salt. Mix well. Bring the mixture to a boil, reduce heat, and let it simmer for 4 hours. Pour the relish into hot, sterile jars and seal them tight. This will make 12 pints of relish.

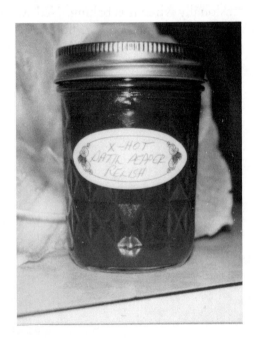

SWEET HOME ALABAMA COLESLAW

2 6-ounce cans evaporated milk
¼ cup sugar
1 teaspoon salt
½ teaspoon pepper
¼ cup vinegar
6 cups finely shredded cabbage

Add the first four ingredients together and mix them well. Slowly add the vinegar, stirring constantly. Cover the mixture and put it in the fridge for about an hour. Pour the dressing over the cabbage and mix that up good. Cover the coleslaw again, and chill it for another hour.

BOY HOWDY HOE CAKES

2 cups cornmeal
1 teaspoon salt
1 cup boiling water
¼ cup cracklings

Mix the cornmeal and salt. Then pour hot water over it while stirring constantly. Blend the dough well and let it cool. Split the cooled dough into 8 pieces and flatten it out. Heat up the cracklings in a heavy cast-iron skillet. Add the hoe cakes and fry them, turning once, until golden brown on both sides.

APPALACHIAN MOUNTAIN BOILED COFFEE

2 cups cold water, divided
1 cup regular coffee grounds
4 eggshells, smashed
6 cups boiling water

Take 1 cup of cold water, and put it with the coffee and eggshells in a big saucepan. Add the boiling water and continue boiling for 5 minutes. Remove the coffee from the heat; add the other cup of cold water and let the coffee stand for 5 minutes. Strain the eggshells out and drink up. The good folks who live in the foothills were kind enough to give me this old family recipe.

Sweet Eats

ST. JOHN'S COUNTY PEACH COBBLER

1 cup milk
1 cup flour, sifted
1 cup sugar
1 large can sliced peaches,
    or 6 freshly sliced peaches
1 teaspoon cinnamon sugar

Mix the milk, flour, and sugar together until the mixture is smooth. Place the peaches in a 2-quart baking dish and pour the mixture over the top of the peaches. Top the cobbler with cinnamon sugar. Bake the cobbler at 350° until golden brown. This is still one of the oldest and best desserts for girlfriends to gossip over. Lord knows they've done it in my family for generations.

IRLEEN'S RUMP DUMP CAKE

1 can of pie filling, any flavor
1 large can crushed pineapple
1 box yellow cake mix, mixed
2 sticks butter, melted
1 cup coconut flakes
1 cup pecans, chopped

Dump all the ingredients in a Bundt pan in the order they are listed above. Bake at 350° for 1 hour. Irleen says, "If ya don't have a rump before eatin' this cake, you'll have one after!"

COOCHIE'S MARSHMALLOW SURPRISE

1 large tub Cool Whip
8 ounces of sour cream
1 can fruit cocktail, drained
1 bag of small marshmallows
¼ cup chopped pecans

Mix them all together. Put them in the icebox overnight and serve cold the next day.

THONOTASASSA MUD PIE

1 cup butter or 2 sticks oleo, creamed
2 cups sugar
2 tablespoons cocoa
4 eggs, beaten one at a time
2 teaspoons vanilla extract
1½ cups sifted flour
1½ cups flaked coconut
1½ cups chopped pecans or walnuts

Grease and flour a 15 by 10-inch pan. Mix together all the ingredients and put them in the pan. Bake the pie at 350° for 30 minutes, or until a toothpick comes out clean. While the pie is warm, top it with a jar of marshmallow cream. Let the pie cool and frost it with Mud Icing.

MUD ICING

½ cup oleo, softened
1 (16-ounce) box powdered sugar
½ cup cocoa
¼ cup evaporated milk
1 teaspoon vanilla

Mix together all the ingredients till smooth. Add more evaporated milk to thin, if necessary.

BACKWOODS COOKIES

1 package semisweet milk chocolate
1 bag Chinese chow mein noodles
½ cup chopped nuts (optional)
½ cup coconut (optional)

Melt your chocolate in a double boiler, or over low heat on the stove. Remove the chocolate from the heat and add the noodles, nuts, and coconut. Stir until all the ingredients are evenly coated. Drop by spoonfuls onto waxed paper. Place the cookies in the fridge to cool. When they harden, then they're ready to eat. White chocolate can be used as well.

MATER SOUP CAKE

1 can tomato soup
1 teaspoon soda
2 tablespoons shortening
1 cup sugar
2 cups flour
1 teaspoon baking powder
1 teaspoon cloves, ground
1½ teaspoons nutmeg
2 teaspoons cinnamon
½ cup raisins

Mix all of these ingredients together and bake in a cake pan in a slow oven at 350° for about 1 hour. Allow the cake to cool. Frost the cake with Mater Soup Icing.

MATER SOUP ICING

1 8-ounce package cream cheese
1 cup powdered sugar
   Pinch of nutmeg

Mix all the ingredients together and ice the cake when it cools.

UNCLE KERMIT'S HERMITS

½ cup shortening
2 cups brown sugar
3 eggs
2 tablespoons milk
4½ teaspoons baking powder
1½ teaspoons cinnamon
½ teaspoon cloves, ground
1 teaspoon salt
3½ cups flour
2 cups raisins

Cream the shortening and sugar; add the eggs and milk. Stir in the dry ingredients and add the raisins. Drop the cookies by the spoonful on a greased cookie sheet and bake them at 375° for 15 minutes.

NELLIE GRAY'S PECAN PIE

1 tablespoon butter
1 cup brown sugar
3 eggs
1 cup white Karo syrup
¼ teaspoon cinnamon
1 cup pecans, chopped
Pinch of salt
1 unbaked pie shell

Cream the butter and sugar. Beat the eggs lightly and throw in the rest of your ingredients. Mix the ingredients well and pour them into an unbaked pie shell. Bake at 450° for 10 minutes. Then reduce heat to 350° and keep baking for another 35 minutes.

MOCK PECAN PIE

¾ cup brown sugar
1 tablespoon butter
1 cup dark corn syrup
3 eggs, beaten
1 cup oats, raw
1 teaspoon vanilla
 Pinch of salt
1 unbaked pie crust

Cream the brown sugar with the butter. Add the corn syrup and beaten eggs. Throw in the raw oats, vanilla, and salt. Mix well and put the filling in a 9-inch pie crust. Follow the same baking recipe as Nellie Gray's Pecan Pie (page 101), or bake until the pie is set.

COUSIN BILLY'S PUMPKIN PIE

  2 8-ounce packages cream cheese
½ cup sugar
  1 teaspoon vanilla
  2 eggs
  1 large can pumpkin purée
1½ cups sugar
  1 teaspoon salt
  2 teaspoons cinnamon
  1 teaspoon ginger
½ teaspoon cloves, ground
  2 5-ounce cans evaporated milk
  2 9-inch unbaked pie shells

Combine the cream cheese, sugar, and vanilla. Add the eggs while mixing. Blend well and set aside. Now, combine the remaining ingredients in a separate bowl. Pour the cream cheese mixture on the bottom of the pie crusts, ½ in each. Pour the pumpkin mixture on top of the cream cheese mixture. Bake the pies at 350° for 1 hour, or until a toothpick stuck in the middle comes out clean.

OSSIE'S JAPANESE FRUITCAKE

¾ pound butter
2 cups sugar
5 eggs
3 cups flour
3 teaspoons baking powder
1 teaspoon allspice
1 teaspoon cinnamon
1 cup white raisins
1 cup nut meats
½ cup milk

Cream the butter, add the sugar gradually, and add 1 egg at a time. Sift the dry ingredients into a bowl: first the flour, then the baking powder, and then the spices. Put the raisins and nuts in a pan. Then dust them with flour and stir them well. Blend the flour-spice mixture into the creamed butter and eggs. Add the milk, nuts, and raisins. Bake the cake at 350° until golden brown. Ice it with the Fruitcake Frosting.

FRUITCAKE FROSTING

3 or 4 lemons (4 if small)
4 or 5 bananas (5 if small)
1 heaping cup of coconut
1¼ cups sugar
1¼ cups water
2 tablespoons cornstarch

Pour the juice of the lemons over the mashed bananas. Heat the coconut, sugar, and water in a pot over medium heat. Let it come to a boil, and thicken it with cornstarch. Put the frosting in between layers, on top, and on the sides of the cake. This recipe will make 3 layers. This is the best cake ever for the holidays.

YADDA MAY'S STRAWBERRY PIE

1 quart fresh strawberries
1 cup sugar
  Pinch of salt
2 tablespoons flour
8 ounces cream cheese
  Milk for consistency
1 baked pie crust

Take the berries, sugar, salt, and flour and cook them over medium heat until thick. Separately mix the cream cheese and a bit of milk to soften the mixture. Then pour the cream cheese mixture in the bottom of an already baked pie crust and add the cooked strawberry mixture. Chill the pie before serving. Yadda May says, "The ladies at our quilting circle just throw a fit over this!"

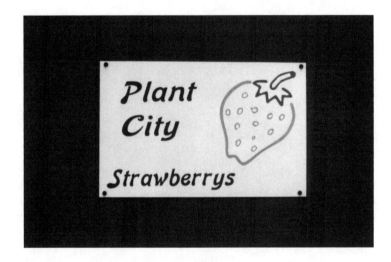

NILLER WAFER CAKE

2 sticks margarine
1½ cups sugar
½ cup milk
6 eggs, beaten
1 box niller wafers
7 ounces flaked coconut
1 cup pecans, chopped

Cream the margarine and sugar. Add the milk and eggs. Break the wafers into small pieces and stir in the coconut, pecans, and wafers. Bake the cake in a tube pan at 300° for 90 minutes.

SWEET POTATO PUDDING

1½ cups milk
4 cups raw sweet potatoes, grated
3 eggs, well beaten
1 cup sugar
Pinch of cinnamon
2 tablespoons flour
¼ cup butter
1 cup shredded coconut
2 teaspoons vanilla
1 small bag marshmallows

Mix all of the above ingredients together. Bake the pudding at 350° for 35 to 45 minutes. When you see that the pudding is close to getting done, you can add marshmallows so they will melt on top.

ORIGINAL BREAD PUDDING

8 slices buttered toast
4 eggs, beaten
½ cup sugar plus 8 teaspoons sugar
2 cups condensed milk
2 teaspoons vanilla
¼ teaspoon salt
1 cup boiling water
⅔ cup seedless raisins
4 teaspoons cinnamon sugar
 Pecans (optional)

Cut each piece of toast into 4 pieces and place the pieces in the bottom of a baking dish. Then mix together the eggs, sugar, condensed milk, vanilla, salt, and 1 cup boiling water. Pour the mixture over the toast. Sprinkle raisins and cinnamon sugar on top. Let it stand for a few minutes to let the bread absorb mixture. Bake at 350° for 45 minutes. Pecans are also good as a topping.

MATTIE BEA'S RICE PUDDING

8 ounces condensed milk
2 eggs
1 cup of cooked rice
¾ cup sugar
2 tablespoons vanilla
  Pinch of salt
1 tablespoon cinnamon

Mix all the ingredients together and bake them in an 8 by 8-inch baking pan at 325° for about an hour, or until firm and golden brown.

OPHELIA'S AMBROSIA BOWL

4 large oranges
4 bananas
1 can pineapple chunks
¼ cup powdered sugar
1 can flaked coconut
¼ cup orange juice
6 maraschino cherries

Peel and slice the oranges and bananas. Drain the syrup from the pineapple chunks and set it aside. Layer the oranges in the bottom of a big bowl and sprinkle them with powdered sugar. Add the pineapple and bananas in 4 alternating layers. Sprinkle coconut over the ambrosia and top with juice and cherries.

SWEET POTATO PIE

4 eggs
1 cup sugar
2 cups sweet potatoes, mashed
Pinch of salt
⅓ cup butter, melted
½ cup evaporated milk
½ teaspoon lemon extract, or 1 teaspoon
    lemon juice
½ teaspoon nutmeg
1 pie shell, unbaked

Beat the eggs until they are light. Add the sugar, sweet potatoes, salt, butter, milk, lemon extract, and nutmeg. Pour the mixture into a pie shell. Bake at 350° for 45 minutes, or until the custard is set.

POOKY LOU'S CHOCOLATE MOO MOOS

2 cups milk
½ cup butter
½ teaspoon cocoa
2 teaspoons vanilla
1 cup crunchy peanut butter
3 cups 1-minute oats

Mix the milk, butter, cocoa, and vanilla in a large pan. Bring to a boil for 3 minutes. Take the pot off the stove and add the peanut butter and oats. Drop the cookies by tablespoons onto waxed paper and let them cool.

If you're having a bad day and everything's going crappy, Grab a cookie, cake, or pie and just be fat and happy.

AUNT FANNIE'S BUTTERMILK PIE

2½ cups sugar
2 tablespoons flour
½ cup butter, softened
1 cup buttermilk
6 eggs, beaten
1 cup flaked coconut
½ cup nuts, chopped
2 unbaked pie shells

Mix the sugar and flour together. Then add butter, buttermilk, and eggs. Mix it well. Add coconut and nuts, and pour it all into 2 unbaked pie shells. Bake for 30 minutes at 350°.

HOMEMADE PECAN LOG

2 cups flour
1 cup sugar
2 teaspoons baking powder
¾ teaspoon salt
½ cup shortening
¾ cup milk
1 teaspoon vanilla
½ teaspoon orange extract
2 eggs
½ cup pecans, chopped

Sift together the flour, sugar, baking powder, and salt. Drop in the shortening. Add ⅔ of the milk and all of the vanilla and orange extract. Then, mix them well. Add eggs and what's left of the milk. Mix that all together. Next, stir in the pecans. Bake the log in a greased and floured pan at 350° for 45 minutes.

DAISY'S FRESH BLUEBERRY PIE

1 package pie crust mix
2 pints fresh blueberries
1 tablespoon lemon juice
1 cup sugar
¼ cup all-purpose flour
1 tablespoon cinnamon
⅛ teaspoon nutmeg
   Pinch of cloves, ground
2 tablespoons butter
1 egg yolk

Make the pie crust as the package directs and shape it in a ball. Divide the ball in half. Put ½ in the fridge until later. Now, on a floured surface, roll out the other half into an 11-inch circle. Use that to line a 9-inch pie plate. Preheat the oven to 400°. Wash the berries. Drain them well, put them in a large bowl, and sprinkle them with lemon juice. Combine the sugar, flour, cinnamon, nutmeg, and cloves. Add them to the berries and mix lightly to combine. Turn the mixture into the pastry-lined pie plate, piling it in the center, and dot with butter.

Roll out the remaining pastry into an 11-inch circle. Make several slits near the center and lay the pastry on the filling. Fold the edges of the top crust under the bottom crust. Press together the edges and crimp decoratively. Beat the egg yolk and a little water. Then brush it lightly over the top crust. Bake the pie 45 minutes, or until the juices start to bubble through the steam holes and the crust is golden. Allow the pie to cool at least 1 hour before serving.

GOOBER PIE

3 eggs
1 cup dark corn syrup
½ cup creamy peanut butter
1 teaspoon vanilla
½ cup sugar
   Pinch of cinnamon
¾ cup peanuts, salted
1 unbaked pie shell

With a mixer, beat the eggs, corn syrup, peanut butter, vanilla, sugar, and cinnamon at medium speed until the mix is smooth and thick. Stir in the nuts and blend. Pour this filling in the pie shell and bake it in a preheated oven at 400°. After about 15 minutes, turn the heat down to 350° and keep baking until the pie is set or a toothpick comes out clean. For the best goober pie, pile some whipped cream on top.

UNCLE BUDDY'S GREEN MATER PIE

2 unbaked pastry crusts
3 cups green tomatoes, sliced
1½ cups sugar
¼ teaspoon salt
5 teaspoons grated lemon zest
¼ teaspoon cinnamon
5 tablespoons lemon juice
¼ cup butter, unsalted

Preheat the oven to 350°. Roll out one unbaked crust and fit it into a 9-inch pie pan. Put a layer of tomatoes in the bottom of the pastry-lined pan. In a bowl, combine the sugar, salt, lemon zest, cinnamon, lemon juice, and butter. Blend these ingredients and pour ⅓ of the mix over the tomatoes already in the bottom of the pie shell. Now, make another layer of tomatoes and repeat. Roll out the top crust and place it over the filling. Pinch the edges and poke holes on top. Bake the pie for 45 minutes, or until it is bubbling and golden brown.

POTATO CHIP COOKIES

1 cup brown sugar
1 cup white sugar
1 cup shortening
2 eggs
2 cups flour
1 teaspoon salt
1 teaspoon baking soda
2 cups potato chips, crushed

Cream the sugars and shortening; stir in the eggs and mix well. Mix together the flour, salt, baking soda, and crushed chips. Then add that to the creamed mixture. Shape the dough into little balls and place them on an ungreased cookie sheet. Mash them down with a fork. Bake at 350° for 10 to 12 minutes.

SOUTHERN CHESS PIE

½ teaspoon salt
3 egg yolks
⅔ cup sugar
1 tablespoon flour
1⅓ cups whipping cream
1 cup dates
1 cup walnuts, chopped
1 teaspoon vanilla
1 unbaked pie crust

Beat together the salt, egg yolks, sugar, and flour. Stir in the whipping cream, dates, nuts, and vanilla. Pour this filling into the pie crust and bake the pie at 350° for 1 hour, or until the crust is golden brown.

ODETTA'S FINGER-LICKIN' APPLE CRISP

½ cup butter, melted
½ cup flour
1 cup oatmeal
¼ cup brown sugar
½ cup water
7 or 8 apples, peeled and sliced

Mix together the butter, flour, oatmeal, and brown sugar. Put water in the bottom of the pan. Then place the apples in the water. Sprinkle the flour mixture over the apples and bake the crisp for 45 minutes at 350°.

LAZY-WOMAN'S CAKE

2 cups sugar
3 cups flour
2 teaspoons baking soda
1 teaspoon salt
5 tablespoons cocoa
1 cup cooking oil
1 tablespoon vanilla
2 tablespoons vinegar
2 cups cold water

In a large bowl, sift together the sugar, flour, baking soda, salt, and cocoa. Make 3 holes in the dry ingredients. Pour the oil, vanilla, and vinegar in each hole; pour water over the whole thing and mix it with a fork until smooth. Bake at 350° for 30 minutes. Now, ain't that the height of laziness?

POOR-MAN'S CAKE

1 cup sugar
1 cup salad dressing
2 teaspoons baking soda
1 cup warm water
2 cups flour
4 tablespoons cocoa
  Pinch of salt
1 teaspoon vanilla

Cream the sugar with salad dressing. Mix the baking soda and water; add it to the creamed mixture. Sift the flour and cocoa. Then stir it into the mixture. Mix in the salt and vanilla. Blend well. Bake at 350° until the cake is golden.

SHOOFLY PIE

¾ cup dark molasses
¾ cup boiling water
½ teaspoon baking soda
¼ teaspoon salt
1½ cups flour, sifted
¼ cup butter
½ cup brown sugar
1 unbaked pie crust

Mix the molasses, water, baking soda, and salt together. Now, with your hands, mix the flour, butter, and brown sugar in a separate bowl. Pour ⅓ of the molasses mixture in the pastry-lined pie pan. Sprinkle with ⅓ of the flour mixture. Continue to alternate the layers, ending with flour mixture on top. Bake the pie at 375° for 35 minutes. This recipe is as old as the hills.

GEORGIA PEACH LEATHER

Peel and pit about 10 Georgia peaches and put them through a sieve. To every 4 cups of pulp, add 1⅔ cups sugar. Mix it all together and bring it to a boil for 2 minutes, stirring constantly. Spread a thin layer on a cookie sheet. Then cover it loosely with a cheesecloth. Dry it in the sun for 3 to 4 days, or until the candy can be rolled like leather. Sprinkle the candy with sugar, cut it in strips, and roll it. Keep it in an airtight container.

PEACH SLUMP

6 cups sliced peaches
1½ teaspoons cinnamon
1 cup sugar
¼ cup evaporated milk
2 tablespoons butter
1 dozen biscuits, unbaked

Mix the peaches, cinnamon, sugar, milk, and butter in a medium-sized pot on the stove. Heat the peach mixture to boiling, then let it simmer. Meanwhile, bake your biscuits as directed on the package. When biscuits are almost done, take them out of the oven and place them in the bottom of a casserole dish. Pour the hot peach mixture over the almost done biscuits. Put the slump in the oven and bake at 350° for about 15 minutes. Eat this with vanilla ice cream. If you're in a slump, this'll drag you right out of it!

PERSIMMON CAKE

1 teaspoon vanilla
1 cup white sugar
½ cup milk
3 eggs, separated
¼ teaspoon cinnamon
2 teaspoons butter, melted
1 teaspoon baking soda
½ cup brown sugar
½ cup pecans, chopped
1 cup flour
¼ teaspoon salt
2 cups persimmon pulp

Mix all the ingredients together, adding the persimmons last. Bake the cake in a tube pan at 350° for 1 hour. This is a very old Southern family recipe and one of my great-grandfather's favorites. Daddy Will affectionately referred to them as "simmerins."

PERSIMMON PUDDING

1 cup flour
¼ teaspoon salt
1 teaspoon baking soda
¼ teaspoon cinnamon
3 eggs, separated
½ cup milk
2 tablespoons butter
1 teaspoon vanilla
½ cup brown sugar
1 cup white sugar
1 cup pecans, chopped
2 cups persimmon pulp

Sift the flour, salt, baking soda, and cinnamon together in a large bowl. Beat the egg yolks and milk. Then add the butter, vanilla, and brown and white sugars to the dry mixture. Add the pecans and persimmon pulp to the dry mix. Now, fold in beaten egg whites and pour the pudding into a large, greased baking pan. Bake the pudding for 1 hour at 350°. When it is cool, cut it into squares and serve.

COLA CAKE

2 cups flour
2 cups sugar
1 cup oleo
2 tablespoons cocoa
1 cup cola
1 teaspoon baking soda
½ cup buttermilk
2 eggs, beaten
1 teaspoon vanilla
¼ teaspoon salt
1 cup mini marshmallows

Sift the flour and sugar into a bowl. Heat the oleo, cocoa, and cola to a boil then pour over the flour mixture. Add the baking soda, buttermilk, eggs, vanilla, salt, and marshmallows. The batter will turn thin, and the marshmallows will float on top. Pour the batter into a greased and floured oblong pan. Bake the cake at 350° for 30 minutes. Be sure to frost the cake with Cola Icing while it's hot.

COLA ICING

½ cup oleo
6 tablespoons cola
2 tablespoons cocoa
1 (16-ounce) box powdered sugar
1 cup pecans, chopped
1 teaspoon vanilla

Mix the oleo, cola, and cocoa. Heat the mixture to a boil. Pour over sugar, add pecans and vanilla. Pour it over your hot cake.

AUNT GONGER'S CHOCOLATE PIE

½ cup semisweet chocolate
½ cup cornstarch
1½ cups sugar
3 egg yolks
1 cup milk
1 cup condensed milk
2 teaspoons vanilla
2 tablespoons butter
2 unbaked pie shells

Mix the dry ingredients and add the egg yolks, milk, and condensed milk. Cook this over medium heat until it is thick. Add the vanilla and butter. Let this mixture cool and pour it into the pie shells. Bake this at 350° until the pie is set. Aunt Gonger always made two of these because one doesn't last very long.

ADEL'S SUGARED PECANS

½ cup butter
2 egg whites
1 cup sugar
   Salt to taste
3 cups pecan halves
   Cinnamon sugar for dusting

Melt the butter in a baking pan. Beat the egg whites until soft peaks form; gradually add the sugar and salt, beating until stiff. Pour in the pecans. Now, add this mixture to the prepared buttered pan. Bake the sugared pecans at 325° for 30 minutes, or until they are brown and all of the butter is absorbed, stirring every few minutes to coat them evenly. Remove them while they are warm, drop them onto waxed paper, and sprinkle cinnamon sugar over the top. Let the pecans cool.

Rugrats and
Curtain Climbers

CHILDREN'S COFFEE

¾ glass of milk
¼ glass of coffee
3 teaspoons sugar

SHUT YER MOUTH PUNCH

5¾ cups pineapple juice
1 cup lemon juice
1 cup sugar
1 pint cranberry juice
2 quarts ginger ale
   Vanilla ice cream

Mix all the ingredients, except for the ginger ale and ice cream. Chill in the fridge for a few hours. Add the ginger ale and ice cream when ready to serve. "If you've got screamin' young 'uns, this'll shut 'em up!" says Onnie Jane of St. Augustine.

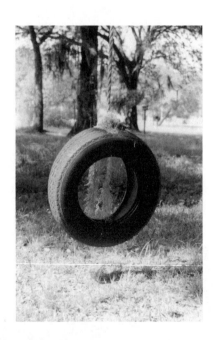

MESS-A-GOO

¼ cup butter
1 cup graham cracker crumbs
¾ cup shredded coconut
1 cup chocolate chips
1 cup pecans, chopped
1 can condensed milk

In an 8 by 8-inch pan, melt the butter. Then sprinkle a layer of graham cracker crumbs. Now layer the other ingredients in the order they're listed above. The milk goes on last, drizzled over the top. Bake the goo for 25 minutes at 350°. Let it cool and cut it into squares. This is Irma Lee's cousin's recipe and she says, "They don't call this a Mess-A-Goo for nothin'!"

NANER PUNCH

Blend 3 naners (bananas) in a blender, add ½ of 1 46-ounce can of pineapple juice, and freeze the mixture.

When it's time to serve, slush the frozen portion and add the remainder of the pineapple juice and 1½ bottles of ginger ale. This makes 1 gallon. Rugrats love this one!

SILLY BILLIES

2 cups brown sugar
1 cup butter, melted
2 eggs, beaten
2 cups self-rising flour
1 cup pecans, chopped
1 teaspoon vanilla

Stir the sugar in with the melted butter. Then, add your eggs, flour, nuts, and vanilla. Lightly stir mixture with a spoon. Bake in two 8-inch pans at 350° for about 20 minutes. Cool and cut into bars.

TUNA PUPPIES

1 can tuna fish
¼ cup chopped celery
¼ cup sweet relish
2 eggs, hard-boiled
½ cup mayonnaise
¼ cup diced sweet onion
   hot dog buns

Mix all the ingredients together and place them on hot dog buns. Warm them in a 350° oven for 10 to 15 minutes.

FERGUS JR.'S POPCORN BALLS

½ stick butter
1 bag mini marshmallows
2 bags unsalted, prepopped popcorn

This is so easy. Melt the butter, and add the marshmallows. Stir until the marshmallows are melted and creamy. Pour the mixture over the popcorn and stir. Wet your hands to keep from getting sticky. Then form a bunch of small balls. Keep wetting your hands and shaking off the excess water as you go. Wrap each ball in colored Saran Wrap or in waxed paper and they'll stay fresh.

TISSIE'S HOMEMADE TURTLES

30 caramel candies
2 tablespoons cream
1½ cups pecans, chopped
6 ounces of chocolate chips

Melt the caramels and add the cream and nuts. Stir until it is mixed up good. Then drop the mixture by spoonfuls onto a cookie sheet. Melt the chocolate chips and drizzle the chocolate over the caramels.

DEWEY ZACK'S CRACK 'EM JACKS

1 stick butter
2 cups brown sugar
1½ cups corn syrup
¼ cup water
1 teaspoon vinegar
1 teaspoon vanilla
1 bag unsalted, prepopped popcorn

Melt the butter in a pan. Stir in the brown sugar, corn syrup, water, vinegar, and vanilla. Bring this concoction to a boil for 5 minutes, being sure not to scorch it. Pour this over the popcorn in a baking dish and bake it for 15 minutes at 350°.

MOO COW

2 scoops vanilla ice cream
2 tablespoons chocolate syrup
¾ cup cold root beer
Cool Whip topping

In a tall glass, stir in 1 scoop ice cream and the chocolate syrup. Mix together. Then pour in the root beer until the glass is half full. Add the rest of the ice cream and root beer. Then fill the glass to the top with Cool Whip. This is dairy good!

MISS BONNIE'S CHOCOLATE GRAVY

¼ cup cocoa
1 teaspoon vanilla
2¼ cups milk
3 tablespoons cornstarch
⅔ cup sugar
Pinch of salt

Mix all the ingredients and bring to a boil. When it gets thick, pour it over your hot, buttered biscuits.

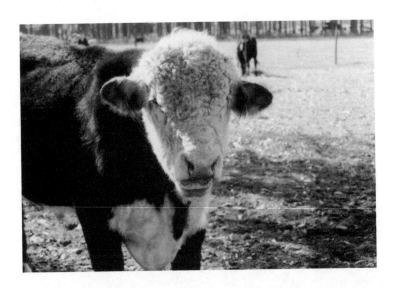

LI'L DEVIL'S ANGEL CAKE

1 angel food cake
1 package Jell-O, any flavor
1 tub of Cool Whip

In a Bundt pan, tear your angel food cake into chunks and layer half of the torn-up cake in the bottom of the pan. Next, make Jell-O as directed on the package. When the Jell-O is almost firm, but still kind of soupy, pour half of it over the cake chunks. Now, take your Cool Whip and put half of that on top of the layers. With the rest of your ingredients, make another layer just like above. Put the cake in the fridge for a couple of hours to let it firm up. "This'll keep them li'l devils busy for a spell!" Mrs. Ima J. Plunkett assured me.

Index

MAIN DISHES

Beef

Chicken and Turkey

Fish, Shrimp, Crab, and Whatever